LAND INVESTMENT:
Guide to a
Second Income Fortune

LAND INVESTMENT:

Guide to a
Second Income Fortune

James H. Dygert

Prentice-Hall, Inc.

Englewood Cliffs, New Jersey

Prentice-Hall International, Inc., *London*
Prentice-Hall of Australia, Pty. Ltd., *Sydney*
Prentice-Hall of Canada, Ltd., *Toronto*
Prentice-Hall of India Private Ltd., *New Delhi*
Prentice-Hall of Japan, Inc., *Tokyo*

© 1976, by

PRENTICE-HALL, INC.

Englewood Cliffs, N.J.

Library of Congress Cataloging in Publication Data

Dygert, James H.
   Land investment.

   Includes index.
   1. Real estate investment. 2. Real estate in-
vestment--United States. I. Title.
HD1375.D84   332.6'324   75-29062
ISBN 0-13-522573-6

Printed in the United States of America.

ABOUT THE AUTHOR

JAMES H. DYGERT has been an active and successful part-time investor in land for many years. Using his system of seeking out raw land on the brink of a sharp value rise, he has built an initial investment of $1,000 into profits and holdings of more than $100,000 and has never sustained a loss on a real estate investment.

Mr. Dygert studied real estate and real estate law while attending the University of Michigan School of Business Administration. He has been a licensed real estate salesman and supervised extensive property holdings and real estate dealings for a diversified corporation while serving as executive assistant to the corporation's president.

An article on his land investment system appeared in *Esquire* magazine. Mr. Dygert is City Editor of the Dayton (Ohio) *Daily News*.

HOW THIS BOOK
CAN MAKE YOU RICH

You don't need big money to make big money in real estate. You also don't need training, experience or luck. All you need is a willingness to learn about an investing technique that's as close to being foolproof as possible, and then go out and use it.

You don't have to be an expert or a gambler. You don't need to be a big shot, belong to a privileged group, or be part of big business. You don't even need a lot of time, or have to contribute a lot of work. With just a little prudent enterprise in your spare time, you can make thousands of dollars in a few years on a small initial investment—possibly even with no money at all.

Your profits can far outstrip anything that's possible in other forms of investment. You can use real estate to make yourself wealthy, independent and secure for the rest of your life. All with very little risk of ever losing a penny.

The trick is to invest astutely in raw land that's about to be in demand for development. This book shows you how it's done, and precisely how you can do it.

You will learn what kind of land offers the best opportunities, where to find it, how to tell when land values are about to rise quickly, and where to get the information you need to choose investments that will make you big profits in a short time.

This book spells out in detail how easy it is to make money in land, why land prices will keep going up, how you can use land investments to turn inflation to your profit, and why it's almost impossible to lose if you exercise ordinary good sense.

If you had bought $1,000 worth of General Motors stock in 1962, it would have been worth about $1,500 in 1972. If you had put it more shrewdly into Eastman Kodak stock instead, you would have made $4,300. By the end of 1974, however, with the stock market at the bottom of a precipitous fall, your profits would have been wiped out. In other stocks, you would have suffered severe losses. Yet, during all that time, land prices kept rising. If you had put that $1,000 into land instead of stock in 1962, you could have made as much as $200,000 in the next 10 to 15 years with almost no risk of losing.

Land in Vermont ski country went from $50 an acre to $3,500 an acre in a ten-year period. Cape Cod property went up more than 300 percent in ten years. Highway frontage north of Detroit that I could have bought for $100 a foot a few years ago was on the market for $1,000 a foot recently. Land in Michigan's Upper Peninsula that I bought for $22,000 increased in value to $50,000 in only two years.

What was out in the country not long ago is now plush suburbia and shopping center territory as America's metropolitan areas keep expanding, with land values 1,000 to 10,000 times higher. What seemed too high five years ago is five times higher today. And now there's an even bigger boom, with faster and sharper price climbs, in vacation, recreation and country land.

And it's just beginning. The price soaring of the past 30 years is just the tuneup for what will happen in the next 50 to 100 years under the impact of ever-increasing demand and other upward pressures on land values—all of which are examined and explained in this book.

It takes very little money or effort to profit from these rising land values. This book tells you exactly how to do it, in easy-to-understand, step-by-step fashion. In 1967, I scraped up $200 and used it as a down payment on a $4,000 purchase of 80 acres in northern Michigan vacation land. Four years later I sold it for $11,000 and used part of the profits to make a down payment on $22,000 worth of land in Michigan's Upper Peninsula that was worth $50,000 two years later. This on a beginning of only $200.

This book shows you how to do the same thing, starting with practically nothing and building it rapidly into thousands of dollars with very little effort—not just once, but over and over again, using your profits from one deal to make several more, multiplying and pyramiding your profits into hundreds of thousands of dollars in just a few years—and have fun while you're doing it.

One does not need to be a genius or a clairvoyant to realize that demand for land, especially vacation property and recreation land, will be on the rise for many years to come. There are more opportunities today than ever before, and there will be even more in the future. This book explains in clear, precise terms how to take advantage of land's inevitable value increase to make big profits.

That land values will keep rising is as close to an investment certainty as you can get. The supply of land never increases, but the demand does—as population and personal wealth keep growing. Real estate is the world's most precious resource, its chief source of wealth and subsistence, and the basis for more personal fortunes throughout history than any other form of investment.

The secret of making a profit quickly is to buy land in the right location, where it's value is likely to rise sharply in the near future—on the fringe of development growth. As John Jacob Astor said years ago, the technique is "to buy on the fringe and wait." As this book makes clear, you don't have to wait very long in modern times if you use the "fringe" secret right. This means, as this book lays out in plain language, buying land that faces an imminent use change because of approaching development, land where development and demand are likely to go next, but where prices are still low.

This book will teach you where to look for ripe fringe areas, how to pick the precise spots with the highest profit potential, and how to buy them at the lowest possible price. It's not difficult, but it is important to go about it properly and patiently in order to buy right—in the right location, under the right conditions, at the right time, and at the right price. This book tells you the precise steps to take.

It also discloses the secrets of maximizing profits with low-price leverage and installment buying leverage. You will learn why it's easy to make bigger profits in $50-an-acre land then $100-an-acre land, how you can triple your return by paying $100 down on a $2,000 purchase instead of paying cash, and how you can heap profits upon profits with compound leverage.

The pitfalls and drawbacks are also described, along with how to avoid them and minimize them—and why you should never buy a lot in a development project no matter how attractive it may look.

You will get down-to-earth guidelines on how and when to sell your land for maximum profit, how to negotiate a top price, how to locate and contact potential buyers, how to sell land before you buy it, how to avoid overextending your resources, and how to make money on land while it pays for itself.

This book also gives you valuable tips on the best kind and sizes of land to buy, the specifics of location and other characteristics that make land most valuable, the rules of zoning and appraisal, the pros and cons of subdividing and packaging, other routes to real estate profits, the advantages of group investing, and the reasons why raw land is the best investment in the world for the small investor—the safest, surest, easiest way there is to make yourself rich.

James H. Dygert

CONTENTS

mounting Obstacles . . . .No Need for High Pressure . . . .The Value of Good
Timing.

One Way to Get Self-Financing Land . . . .A House on a Hot Spot . . . .More
Income, More Problems . . . .Pros and Cons of Dealing in Houses . . . .How
to Make Leverage Work with Houses . . . .Easy to Buy, Easy to
Sell . . . .Advantages and Risks of a Long-Term Approach . . . .Profits and
Pitfalls in Apartments . . . .The Extra Profits in Depreciation Tax
Shelters . . . .A Few Tax Shelter Figures and How They Work . . . .Enlarging
the Tax Shelter with Leverage . . . .A Couple of Catches, However . . . .A
Few Words of Caution . . . .Losing Money on No Investment at All . . . .The
Difficulties of Controlling Costs . . . .The Uncertainties of Income
. . . .Opportunities in Slum Properties—Unsavory and Other-
wise . . . .The Risky New Fad in Condominiums . . . .Opportunities in Com-
mercial and Industrial Income Property . . . .Raw Land Still the Best Bet.

A Way to Get in on Bigger Deals Faster . . . .The Other Side of the Group
Coin . . . .Simple and Complicated Partnerships . . . .Advantages and Drawbacks of the Limited Partnership . . . .Improving the Odds by Including
the Influential . . . .The High-Powered Approach Called Syndication . . . .Investing in Corporate Fashion . . . .Congenial Group Investing Through an Informal Club . . . .The New Fad—Real Estate Investment Trusts . . . .Three Kinds of REITs . . . .A Brief Look at One Small
REIT . . . .Now, the Bad News about REITs . . . .Distinguishing Good
Groups from Bad Groups.

When to Use an Option to Get the Best Odds . . . .Using Options as a Route to
Rezoning Profits . . . .The Real Estate Listing as an Option . . . .No-Cost
Options and Other No-Risk Gambits . . . .A Variety of Uses and Big Profits
with No Risk . . . .Tactics for No-Money-Down Investments . . . .Double
Borrowing for No-Cash Deals . . . .A Combination Maneuver to Buy With
No Money . . . .Opportunities at Rock-Bottom Prices . . . .Good Buys from
Our Largest Landowner, Uncle Sam . . . .Selling Land to the Gov-
ernment . . . .Something for the Adventurous Types.

The Easiest Path to Wealth and Security . . . .An Investment for the Mod-
ern-Day Individualist . . . .Building a Fortune as a Part-Time Pursuit . . . .Why Real Estate Is the Best Investment . . . .Why Raw Land Is

1

BIG PROFITS
ON LITTLE MONEY

A wealthy Detroit industrialist named Jim Robbins emerged briefly in the news a few years ago as a potentially important figure in a management scandal that was convulsing the Chrysler Corp. Robbins basked in a spotlight of attention for a few weeks as the news media reported that he might lead a proxy fight to take control of Chrysler's board of directors and clean up the mess. Actually, Robbins never seriously intended to make such a move, since he knew he had insufficient backing, but the opportunity for glamorous publicity was too inviting to ignore.

It was typical of Robbins to appear to be something he wasn't. Though known as the millionaire head of a far-flung, diversified business empire who built race cars for the Indianapolis 500 and flew a two-engine Aero Commander from the airstrip alongside his headquarters in the Detroit suburb of Troy, Robbins was not the successful industrialist, manufacturer or businessman he appeared to be.

The Secret Behind One Man's Millions

His "empire" was, to a large extent, an illusion. It consisted of a plastics molding factory, two smaller shops, an airplane distributorship, a retail sporting goods store, a golf course and restaurant, and a golf driving range. Most of these operations were in the red in the early 1960's. Robbins actually was making his money in land—vacant land he had astutely bought in the path of the rapid suburban growth in the 1950's.

Robbins was a shrewd trader who bought cheap and sold dear. He had an instinct for timing and an intuition for a seller's desperation. He never bought unless the price was absurdly low. He applied his talent to everything from executive jets to paper clips, but nowhere with more spectacular profit than in real estate. I know this because in 1961 I was his executive assistant and among my duties was looking after his real estate interests. It was there, in fact, that I learned for the first time some key secrets of profitable land investment.

Near the end of World War II, Robbins used some connections at Chrysler Corp., where he had been employed prior to the war, to get a new car dealership in a Detroit suburb. With the huge profits he reaped from the explosion of demand for new automobiles in the postwar years, he bought raw land in undeveloped suburban areas north of Detroit.

This was just before America's great postwar exodus to suburbia. Land was cheap. Then, as the suburban expansion began, Robbins started selling his land at enormous profits. He used the proceeds to buy still more land farther out from the city where prices were still low because development had not yet reached out that far. Many people who lived in what then seemed "out in the country," but which today are bustling suburbs, made lots of money just on luck. I know of some who bought small farms 15 miles out from the city at prices like $20,000 for 40 acres and an old frame house, then sold a few years later to developers for $5,000 an acre. But Robbins wasn't being lucky. He knew exactly what he was doing. His tactic of buying raw land a bit ahead of development, then cashing in when development hit, is the same one that has made thousands of dollars for me and can do the same for you. The buying and selling of strategically located raw land is the quickest, easiest, most foolproof way there is to make big money on investments.

An example of how to do it is one purchase that Robbins made, a parcel that had half a mile of frontage on a main road five miles north of Detroit. One end of the parcel was on a corner with another main road. Within just a few years, Robbins sold the corner—only a small fraction of the entire parcel—for more than he had paid originally for the entire parcel. He later got the remainder rezoned for industrial use and subdivided it into lots. When I was working for him, one of my duties was to sell these lots for $150 to $200 per front foot. Since Robbins had already sold the corner for more than his original investment, every penny was profit. Actually, he never invested the full price in the first place, since he had made a small down payment and a few subsequent payments on a land contract. When he sold the corner, he paid off the contract and owned the rest free and clear. Robbins profited handsomely on many deals like that in raw land. He undoubtedly would have become a multi-millionaire on his land dealings alone if he hadn't been killed in a plane crash a few years ago.

No Need for Big Money

When I left Robbins' employ I figured that one thing I had learned from him was that it was smart to invest carefully in land. However, that was only the beginning of my education. It's said that a little knowledge can be a dangerous thing, and in my case it was—not in the usual sense of leading me to make a rash move, but in causing me to be hesitant and overly cautious in my relative ignorance. I played it too safe, and thereby lost out on good chances to make lots of money. I didn't buy any land for awhile, even though just about any real estate that I could have bought then would have brought me big profits in less than five years. But I thought I couldn't invest because I didn't have any money, and that was a costly mistake.

It's easy to fall into that wrongheaded kind of thinking. Money, after all, can and does make more money. Names in American history associated with wealth and land—Astor, Vanderbilt, Carnegie, Rockefeller—first made their money in industry or finance and then bought land. Land development today is a $6-billion-a-year big business, and most of it is controlled by a few large corporations. Several industrial giants, including auto manufacturers, steel firms, oil companies and such others as ALCOA, Boise Cascade, DuPont, General Electric, International Paper, and International Telephone and Telegraph, are into land development in a big way. Many also have purchased huge chunks of undeveloped real estate to be held for appreciation in value. All big money. Most people who have made millions in real estate got money from other sources before making any in real estate. That was true of Robbins, and is true today of movie stars, sports heroes, other celebrities, doctors, lawyers and businessmen who invest in real estate.

So, it's not surprising that it might look discouragingly unavoidable that one needs a lot of money to get started in real estate investment. But that simply is not true. It's just an illusion. And that's one of the first things you must understand if you are to make money in land without first waiting to get a large inheritance or a sudden bundle from some magic source.

The fact is that you can start with practically no money at all. You can apply the principle of using other people's money, use the same tactics that Robbins and other real estate millionaires have employed, and make thousands of dollars in a few years—if you operate carefully, intelligently and patiently. One reason why raw land is the best investment in the world is that it's usually the least expensive land you can buy. That makes it the easiest to buy without much money or resources to start with. There are many kinds of real estate, many other ways to profit in real estate, and even many other types that can be bought with small initial investments, but none offers greater potential return or less risk than well-located raw land. And none is easier to start buying than inexpensive raw land that is certain to be in demand for development in the near future.

$6,000 Profit on a $200 Plunge in Only Four Years

This is not quite as true about land in the path of suburban expansion as it used to be, since prices are higher on everything everywhere, including farmland just a few miles from growing metropolitan areas. But it is still true—and will continue to be for many years to come—in regard to the second, more recently emerged area of spectacular opportunity for big profits in raw, soon-to-be-developed land; namely, vacation and recreation land. This, in fact, is where the lowest prices and best chances for big profits are available today, and will be available for the foreseeable future.

There's a good illustration of that in my own experience. After I came to realize that I didn't need a lot of money to make money in land, I bought an 80-acre tract in northern Michigan for $4,000, with only $200 as a down payment. It was located on a blacktopped county road about five miles from Kalkaska, then a quiet, rustic, trout-fishing village not yet touched by feverish resort development. But it was only 25 miles from a busy, fast-growing vacation area around Grayling, about the same distance from the expanding resort areas around Traverse City, and about 50 miles from Houghton Lake, one of Michigan's most overdeveloped recreation and resort locations.

My idea was to invest where prices had not yet been driven up by a development boom, but where the boom might well go in the not-too-distant future. The boom did indeed reach Kalkaska—even sooner than I had hoped. Within four years, I had sold my 80 acres for $11,000 cash. This was $137.50 an acre, almost triple the $50 an acre I had paid. After paying a $1,000 commission to a real estate agent, I had a net price of $10,000—a $6,000 profit. Pretty nifty for an initial investment of only $200 and modest monthly payments for four years. The total I paid out over four years, including taxes and interest, was $3,915—not quite equal to the original price. Counting everything, I almost tripled my money in only four years.

This is but one example of how you can use the secret of strategic land investment for your own big profit even though you may have only a few dollars to start with.

No Experience Necessary, Either

Real estate is the world's chief source of subsistence and wealth. It's been the basis for more personal fortunes throughout history than any other form of investment. Land is our most precious resource. Still, very few people buy real estate as an investment for profit.

Most investment in American real property is done by big corporations, financial institutions, insurance companies, wealthy businessmen, people in the real estate business, doctors, lawyers, sports stars and others with oversized incomes looking for a tax shelter.

Although the stirrings of a new trend toward real estate investments among individual investors began to be evident in the early 1970's, mostly because of inflation and the stock market's disastrous plummeting, most individual investors in the past have avoided real estate, apparently on the mistaken notion that it's too much trouble. Home ownership is technically an investment and many Americans are homeowners who hope to make a profit if they have occasion to sell. But their main purpose is not to invest for profit, but to have a home of their own. The recent rush to buy lots in big vacation-land developments is part of the growing new interest in real estate and to a great extent has been promoted by pitches about investment and profit, but the motivation of buyers is still primarily to have a place of their own where they can go for rest, relaxation and recreation.

The average investor seldom thinks of real estate as a type of investment for profit that he can handle or feel comfortable about. He usually thinks instead of the stock market, which in reality is far riskier and almost always less profitable. According to Larry J. Fortman, head of a real estate financial and development firm and two real estate investment trusts in Columbus, O., most investors do not want to take the time or trouble to give close attention to their investments. They like to invest with the ease and dispatch of a phone call to their broker, and prefer to rely on their broker's expertise and advice rather than learn the ropes themselves. There seem to be too many details to learn and manage. They assume their lack of experience is too big an obstacle and therefore it would be too much work and too little fun.

There always seem to be a few who have the luck or magic foresight to see the potential in an area like Phoenix, Ariz., or the Florida coast long before everyone else. But their success is often not a matter of luck or mystery at all. They merely took the time and made the effort to learn some key facts about real estate and the tricks of profitable investing, even though they may not have had prior experience in real estate. It is true that people in the real estate field are better able to recognize and take advantage of good investment opportunities, but it's not necessary to work in real estate to learn enough for buying and selling at a profit. You can quickly learn the main secrets of effective land investing, and then get the feel of using them just by going out and doing it.

Not Nearly So Hard As It Might Look

You don't need big money or a lot of expertise. You don't have to become a developer or a big time operator or a member of a real estate establishment or investment clique. You can be just an individual investor who goes quietly and carefully about using the opportunities and techniques made available by America's free enterprise economic system to get off the treadmill of wages and expenses. You can operate on a small scale, yet make big profits that will make you and your family comfortable and secure in a way that working for a living rarely achieves by itself. You can buy and sell raw land with almost no risk of ever losing a penny and make thousands of dollars within a few years without investing much money, time or effort. If the only thing that holds you back is a fear that it's too complicated, too difficult, or too time-consuming, the first thing you have to do is get that nonsense out of your head. The truth is that it's easy. Once you learn a few basic ground rules, it's not hard at all. It can even be a lot of fun.

The Importance of a Right Attitude

It's a matter of attitude as well as technique. You must have a willingness and determination to succeed as well as self-confidence in your ability to learn and apply the concept of strategic buying—which means buying right, in a right place, under right conditions, at the right time, and at a right price.

Attitude is crucial to the successful use of strategic buying. You must be unhurried, careful, patient, sure of what you are doing. You must persist in finding the right land to buy before you put up any money or sign any papers. Never get overanxious, no matter how good a buy you believe you've found. Never commit yourself to a purchase until you investigate thoroughly and are convinced on the basis of facts, not promises or persuasive words, that it is undisputedly a right buy. It's not the plan that you get caught up in headlong land mania or get carried away in the great new American land rush, but that you profit from the rush by operating with great care and precision. On the other hand, you must not become so timid and overcautious that you become paralyzed; you must act decisively on the facts.

Such confidence comes from learning the basic rules and proceeding to apply them carefully, learning more as you go. This is not difficult, either, despite the lack of help or encouragement you will probably encounter, which is one reason it's easy to fall into the mistaken thought that real estate is too tough.

Overcoming the Lack of Help

Most books and magazine articles about investing deal with the stock market, as if to say, by ignoring real estate, that it's too complex for you, reserved for the already well-heeled, or otherwise out of your league.

There are mountains of statistics, research and analysis to assist, or confuse, the stock market fancier, but hardly any to help the realty investor. Economists and statisticians don't seem very interested in real estate. What data has been collected is practically impossible to find, or get access to, unless you're in some phase of the real estate business.

The few books that are available on real estate investing tend to emphasize apartments, condominiums and other kinds of improved real estate rather than vacant land, even though raw land affords the biggest profits and the smallest risks. Some even say investing in raw land is too risky, though that's true only when it's done recklessly.

The lack of information and advice on realty investing not only creates the misleading impression that it's difficult, it also leaves you with little help. Nevertheless, it does not require a great deal of time and effort to learn enough to make big money in raw land on your own. Go to the library and read books on real estate, or talk to real estate people you know. You might even be able to take a class or two at a nearby college or adult education course. What you need to do most of all is to get out and start looking for a good buy, with a determination to learn as you go, get help or advice when you need it, and conquer the problems and difficulties as they arise.

Real estate agents can be helpful and you can use their services to your advantage, but you do not always need them, especially when buying. It's not difficult to operate successfully without them, and relying on them too much can hinder your learning of important facts and methods for yourself.

Though most real estate salesmen try sincerely to serve both buyers and sellers, sometimes they lose perspective in their eagerness for a commission. Sometimes they spout persuasive spiels on the wisdom of investing in real estate, while actually talking only about the specific property they are trying to sell and insisting that is the only good investment available. Some might recommend against vacant land because they are selling apartments. The important thing to remember is that you are the one who should decide what to buy and how much to pay, not a salesman. Decisions should be made on the basis of facts, not according to the blandishments of salesmen or your eagerness for profit.

A Few of the Main Secrets and Guidelines

1. Location is all important. There's a lot of land for sale that you don't want to buy. The key element in spotting land that is most likely to come into demand soon and experience sharp rises in value is determining if the location generally is an area where development is headed, and if the specific location will make it highly desirable when that development arrives. It's not always possible to get advance inside information on where a new shopping center is going to be built, but it's not hard to find out generally where a shopping center will be needed, where a vacation area development is likely, or where other potentially valuable land can be found.

2. The biggest jumps in land value occur when usage is about to change, or potential use changes. The sharpest jump of all takes place when land is transformed, or is expected soon to be transformed, from non-use to use, such as when a remote mountain tract suddenly becomes desirable as resort property, or an abandoned farm becomes recognized as a good spot for a suburban apartment complex. This is why raw land offers the biggest profits. The next biggest jump occurs in development or potential development for residential, recreation, industrial or commercial use—or in a change or potential change to a "higher"

(more profitable) use, such as from residential to commercial, or single family residential zoning to multiple family residential. Both of these causes for value jumps are behind the wisdom of buying in the path—or on the "fringe"—of development. To buy after development or a zoning upgrade takes place is to buy after further usage change is unlikely and most of the profit has been milked by someone else. Developed land often does continue to increase value, but practically never as sharply, as fast, or as inevitably as raw land. Companies that peddle lots in developments never mention this.

How to Make Profits Bigger with Leverage

3. Always buy cheap. First, don't pay the asking price or the market price for land unless its location, other characteristics and prospects for quick profit are extraordinary. The object is to get the lowest price possible. If you buy a piece of land for less than its current market value, you don't have to wait at all to make a profit; you just sell it at the going price. Secondly, the best way to make big money in land is with the leverage you get from low prices. If you buy 100 acres at $25 an acre and the price increases by $25 an acre to $50, selling for $5,000 doubles your money. But if you pay $100 an acre and the price increases by $25 an acre, your investment return is only 25 percent. In the first case, you needed only $2,500 to make $2,500. In the second case, it takes $10,000 to make $2,500. Or, if you have only $2,500 to invest, you can buy 100 acres and make 100 percent if you pay only $25 an acre and the price doubles. But if you buy at $100 an acre, you can get only 25 acres and make only $625 when the price goes up by $25.

4. Invest as little money as possible. Use other people's money by purchasing on a land contract with a small down payment. This gives you another kind of leverage. If you actually paid out only $1,000 in down payment and subsequent payments on that $2,500 purchase of 100 acres at $25 an acre, your $2,500 profit when the price rose to $50 an acre would be 250 percent of your investment, not just 100 percent. In that case, you need only $1,000 to make $2,500, and not all of it at the time of purchase. Or, if you have $2,500 to invest, you can buy $10,000 worth on contract and when its value doubles you make $10,000. Buying raw land on a land contract is similar to buying improved property—houses, apartments, other buildings—on a mortgage. Instead of paying the full price, you borrow from a bank or spread the payments to the seller over a period of future time, which is the same as borrowing the money from the seller.

Lots of Land, Time and Opportunity

5. There's plenty of land and opportunity still left, and there will be for many years. Demand for land can't help but continue to grow, perhaps even faster than ever, under the impact of a growing population and the expanding

desires of an increasingly affluent society. Despite the fact that the supply of land is constant, there are still millions of unused, undeveloped acres that can be bought cheap before that growing demand reaches them. To think it's too late would be a grievous and costly error causing you to miss out on profits you could easily gain. But also, don't make the mistake of rushing to buy carelessly in fear that opportunity is fast running out. There's plenty of time to be patient and sure. If you fail to get one piece of land because you don't move quickly enough or the price is too high, just go out and find another. Good investments may not be lying around for you to trip over, but they're not hard to find, either, if you know how to look and make the effort. You haven't missed the good deals; there are still lots of them out there. You need only find them.

No Need for Luck, Either

Land is such a solid investment, a resource that can be expected with certainty to increase in value sooner or later, that even the dumb-luck approach sometimes works. There are a number of rich people who have proven that. But you don't need luck, and many who may have appeared to be lucky actually made their own luck. They weren't dumb at all. Arthur Vining Davis, who made millions by buying up Florida land before it became so popular, didn't just fall into it by chance. He knew it would make him lots of money; he just didn't know how long it would take.

When plans were disclosed in 1967 for a multi-million dollar shopping mall south of Dayton, Ohio, it was revealed that three executives of two big manufacturing firms owned the 120 acres where it would be built, plus another 280 acres nearby. These executives didn't just happen to be in the right place for such a bonanza. It was no accident at all. They had realized six years earlier that a major shopping center would be needed in the fast-growing suburbs south of Dayton. They picked a likely corner located on two state highways and began buying the land. After a while, they began contacting developers and department store officials, giving them sales pitches on the desirability of their site. They had nothing to lose. They knew that even if no shopping center was built on their land, it would still be a highly profitable investment. The moral of this story is that, while luck is nice and it wouldn't be smart to spurn any that happens along, you don't need luck to find a piece of land that you can be sure will increase in value soon.

Better Than Polaroid Stock or IBM

If you had possessed enough luck or clairvoyance to invest $1,000 in Polaroid stock in 1938, it would have been worth about $3,000,000 in 1972. But if you had put that same amount in land on the outskirts of a big city, along the California coast, on a lake in northern Michigan, in the mountains of North

Carolina, Tennessee or Pennsylvania, in the desert outside Las Vegas, Nev., or Phoenix, Ariz., or in any of several other places that today are bustling suburbs or crowded resorts, it could well have been worth up to $10,000,000. That is, if you had paid the full price for the land. If you had paid only a fraction as a down payment, the leverage would have enabled you to do even better. I don't know of anyone who actually did that well, but I'm sure someone did, because it would have been arithmetically possible based on the increases in value in some areas. And you wouldn't have needed mystic foresight to have perceived the wisdom of putting your money in land, just as you don't need it today. All you need is some prudent enterprise.

If you had invested $1,000 in Polaroid, IBM, Xerox, Eastman Kodak, Sears Roebuck, or General Motors stock in 1962, your investment would have been worth from $1,500 to $5,000 in 1972. But if you had used that money to buy $1,000 worth of land, it would have been possible, based on rises in land values, for you to have made $200,000. If you had used the $1,000 as a down payment on $5,000 or $10,000 worth of land back in 1962, you could have made as much as a million dollars in the next ten years. If you had kept any of that stock until 1974, you would have made no money at all and might even have lost some. But land prices kept right on rising. Profits and opportunities became bigger and better than ever.

You don't need a lot of knowledge or expertise to get started. You don't need luck or a lot of money. If you can borrow $500, you don't need any money at all. You don't need to put in a great deal of time and effort, and it can be a lot of fun rather than hard work or drudgery. Investing in land is a great way to combat inflation. All you need is a willingness to learn a few basic facts, go out and get at it, and proceed carefully and sensibly. Best of all, land is the safest investment in the world.

2

WHY YOU CAN'T GO WRONG WITH STRATEGIC BUYING

America's most famous folk hero, Will Rogers, is supposed to have said, "Buy land. They ain't making any more of the stuff."

According to another story, a rich Texan once said, "They're making more people, but they aren't making any more land."

Larry J. Fortman, president of Investors Companies, Inc., a Columbus, Ohio, real estate and development firm, says, "There's just no way you can make more land. So it's impossible for it to go anywhere but up. There's no way you can lose. You can explain this to people, but they don't believe it."

The fact that the land supply cannot be increased is the basic reason why land is the safest, as well as the most profitable, investment you can make. Demand keeps increasing, but supply can't. So values always go up eventually. There's no indication that demand will stop growing in the foreseeable future. Even swampland and desert will become usable and valuable sooner or later.

Why Speculation Is the Wrong Word

Buying raw land in hope of making a profit from its appreciation in value is often called speculation, rather than investment. But that's not the right word for careful, strategic buying. The risk of losing is practically zero—much smaller than in any other kind of investment—if you go about it sensibly and calmly. You don't have to be brilliant; just able to use good judgment and follow reliable guidelines. It's just about impossible to lose unless you buy blindly or hastily.

Of course, things can go wrong with the cleverest of plans. Unforeseen events can upset the most meticulous of arrangements or calculations. It is possible that a person who does everything right could still lose money because of an unanticipated development, or that a person who thought he did everything right turns out later to have miscalculated. Nothing is perfect or 100 percent certain.

But investing wisely in raw land is as close to certainty as you can get. The chances of something's going wrong are smaller in land investment than in any other kind of investment—except ordinarily a government-insured savings account, which is far less profitable and not totally foolproof, either, since you can end up with a loss if the inflation rate is higher than the interest you get. All other kinds of investment—stocks, mutual funds, bonds, commodity futures, jewelry, paintings, rare coins, antiques, other types of real estate, and business enterprise—entail much greater risk than raw land.

The Safety in Stability

Land for the most part is free of sharp, short-term price fluctuations. Even when a boom is driving prices up fast, or when values are nosediving from inflated levels caused by overexcited promotions, the changes are far less abrupt than the price swings, say, in the stock market. Average land values in the United States increased more than 100 percent over a recent 12-year period, while the stock market had no net increase at all. The Dow Jones average for 30 industrial stocks, the market's best known barometer, was the same in 1974 as it was in 1962. Besides, land values were far more stable all during that period. The stock market was zigzagging up and down over those 12 years, once soaring over the 1,000 mark before plunging back down below 600. Meanwhile, land values were moving in only one direction: up.

Real estate is not sensitive to the headlines of the day like the stock market. Rumors can plunge stock investors into fits of enthusiasm or fright and make the market look like a yo-yo. But real estate is impervious to such things. One cannot invest in the stock market on an average basis—despite an attempt to do so by mutual funds—but must buy individual stocks, which rise and fall in value even more crazily than the Dow Jones average. You can't invest in land on an average basis either, of course. You buy a specific piece of land just as you buy shares of stock in a particular corporation. The smaller risk is even more obvious here. A piece of land is just about always more stable in value than a share of stock.

The Predictability of Land Values

The value of a particular stock is far more unpredictable, far more subject to irrational forces and short-term upsets, than a parcel of land. This is true regardless of your knowledge and astuteness, how thoroughly you investigate before you buy, or how intelligently and shrewdly you trade. With land, you can know with a high degree of certainty whether the price will rise soon, if you apply caution and good sense. You know that the value of land will inevitably go up, and the trick is to buy land whose value will rise sooner rather than later. Not only is there no guarantee that a stock will rise in value or price, but its value can drop—and often does. It can even become totally worthless, a catastrophe that almost never befalls land.

Studies have shown that 78 to 92 percent of stock market investors end up losing money. One study, which dealt with the performance of 54 mutual funds, disclosed that the average investor fared worse than if he had put his money in a savings account. Gambling casino employees in Las Vegas once refused to invest their profit-sharing fund in the stock market because they considered stocks too big a gamble. Land, by comparison, is a sure thing.

The Astounding Boom in Land Prices

Land values, except for an occasional brief interlude for an economic depression, have been on the rise steadily for more than three hundred years—ever since the Industrial Revolution brought the world into the modern age of science and technology. Since then, land values have acted like advances in science and technology—increasing at an ever-faster rate. Property prices have been rising especially fast since World War II, booming right along with America's rapidly expanding economy and technology.

Land that sold for $3 an acre in the 1940's turned into a posh residential area in Phoenix worth $25,000 an acre within only ten years. Property in Vermont ski country that was selling for $50 an acre in the early 1960's was bringing up to $3,500 an acre in the early 1970's. What was out in the country 20 years ago is now plush suburbia, with land values 1,000 and 10,000 percent higher, depending on whether current use is residential, industrial or commercial. Land around Cape Cod went up more than 300 percent in one 10-year period. What cost $15 an acre in Palmdale, Calif., in 1950 was worth $8,000 an acre and more in the 1970's. Highway frontage that I could have bought in a suburban area north of Detroit for $100 a foot a few years ago was on the market recently for $1,000 a foot. Residential acreage in that area rose from $1,000 an acre in 1960 to more than $6,000 an acre, and land rezoned for commercial use is up to $200,000 an acre.

In the 20 years from the 1950's to the 1970's, the price of land in developing areas increased an average of 400 to 500 percent. The price of one parcel near Disney World in Florida zoomed from $9,500 per acre to $25,000 an acre in just several months. Land near Kalkaska, Mich., where I sold 80 acres for $137.50 an acre in 1971, was recently priced from $600 to $1,000 an acre. "It keeps going up," one real estate agent there told me. "I don't know where it's going to stop."

Farmland in the United States rose 107 percent in average value from 1959 to 1972 as the land boom hit the nation's rural areas, too, converting farms to housing developments and shopping centers. Farmland recently increased in value an average of 13 percent across the country in only one year, according to figures published by the U.S. Department of Agriculture.

Why the Land Boom Will Go On and On

Opportunity for profits from rising land values is greater and more plentiful than ever. Growth and development, rather than being over or tapering off, promises to be bigger and faster than ever in the next 25 to 50 years. There's no sign that the upward movement in land values will slow down in the foreseeable future. The signs, on the contrary, indicate that all the pressures driving land values up will continue, and perhaps increase, for many years to come. Such developments as the energy crisis and high gasoline prices might dampen the rate of increase occasionally, but the impact will be only temporary.

America keeps growing. Suburbia continues to expand into exurbia. Giant development firms and individual developers keep opening up new subdivisions and starting "new towns" all over the country, even during economic slumps. New shopping malls and suburban office complexes keep sprouting up in metropolitan areas. Americans keep exhibiting an insatiable appetite for more space to live and play. Recognition of land as a good investment is growing, too, which adds another upward push on values. Some developers and promoters use an unscrupulous get-rich-quick pitch to exploit careless buyers with exorbitant prices for inferior land; but the careful investor can sidestep the pitfalls and benefit from the upward pressure put on land prices by fast-buck operators.

15 Reasons for a Future of Rising Land Values

Many real estate experts say there is no reason to expect the land boom to slow down soon. They expect demand and values to keep surging for at least another 50 years. Some believe that a continued rise in land prices for the next century is perhaps the most reliable prediction that can be made about the future of America's economy. These predictions are based mostly on the following factors:

1. Inevitable population increases;
2. Economic growth;
3. An increasing need for more parks and public recreation space;
4. A constantly growing need for more housing and jobs;
5. Continuing increases in personal income, leisure time, and living standards;
6. A still expanding desire among city dwellers to move to the suburbs;

7. A newly emerging ambition of suburbanites to move farther out from the city;

8. A growing desire to own a second home for vacation, recreation or retirement purposes;

9. The easy accessibility of financing in America's credit-oriented economy;

10. The deductability of mortgage and land contract interest on the federal income tax;

11. Encouragement of land ownership and investment by the capital gains provisions of federal income tax laws that tax land profits less than wages and other income;

12. Federal government programs designed to spur incentive toward certain types of construction and investment in real estate with tax shelter opportunities, usually based on depreciation.

13. The flow of foreign money into American real estate as other nations develop.

14. The apparent inevitability of continuing inflation.

15. Increasing government control of land use.

Population Growth and Metropolitan Growth Pressures

Frightening forecasts of exploding population and disastrous overcrowding on scarce land in America are now known to have been exaggerated. Though population growth and birth rates remain high in other countries, the rate of population increase in America is slowing down. The birth rate in the United States has been declining since 1957 and in 1974 fell below the level needed to sustain Zero Population Growth. Young adults want fewer children than they did 20 years ago. The population continues to grow despite that low birth rate because even at that rate there are more births every year than deaths. This happens because there is an unusually large proportion of the population in their twenties, due to the "baby boom" produced by high birth rates from 1945 to 1956.

So, while the population grows, it's not growing as fast as it was once expected. Experts figure the growth will continue for another 50 years, even if the birth rate remains low. The children born between 1965 and 1976 to "baby boom" parents will produce another bumper crop of babies between 1985 and 1996, and these children will do likewise 20 years after that. It will take at least 50 years for all this to level off—longer than that if the birth rate goes up again for any reason.

What this means to you and me as investors is that the demand for land will continue to grow and spread across the country as the number of people who live in the United States increases.

More Land per Person

And that's only part of it. Not only is the number of people increasing who need land, but so is the amount of land each person wants. Demand for land is expanding even faster than the population.

The post-World War II flight to suburbia is going stronger than ever. The yearning of Americans to own a home on a plot of land with room for their children to play outdoors—a piece of earth all their own away from the congestion and dirt of the city—has not diminished in the least. If anything, it is stronger than ever, and there are still millions of city dwellers yet to realize that dream. While suburban growth continues to spread outward in practically every metropolitan area across the United States, efforts by government and private interests to bring the economically and socially disadvantaged into the mainstream of middle class life have only begun to take effect. As the results of these efforts gain impact, more and more city residents will have the resources to realize their desires for the suburban living they have for so long envied—this despite programs by cities to keep people there with grandiose but misdirected rehabilitation schemes. Suburbanites, in turn, will keep moving farther out to bigger lots and fancier houses, constantly expanding the frontiers of suburbia. It's already not uncommon for people to commute to a city job from 50 miles out in exurbia.

Spiraling Desires, Affluence and the New American Dream

Perhaps the most potent force behind the burgeoning demand for land is the new, updated version of the American dream. The more people have, the more they want. Those with a nest of their own in suburbia now want to own a second home, too—a vacation retreat in the north woods, on the seashore, or in the mountains. Despite high taxes and inflation, Americans are more affluent than ever and have more time on their hands. They're spending more and more money and time on leisure activities, recreation, and sports. In recent years they've also grown to want their own land for these purposes.

People are so eager to buy a piece of vacation paradise that hundreds of development firms and fly-by-night promoters are exploiting their gullibility to make millions of dollars a year.

The senior citizen population is also growing, which pushes up the demand for land to be used for retirement homes. In modern, mobile America, the elderly no longer plan on living out their twilight years with their children. They need and want places of their own.

American affluence keeps the demand rising for ski resorts, boat marinas, fishing lakes, swimming areas, snowmobile trails, amusement parks, tourist gimmicks, motels, automobiles, and plane tickets. But most of all, it keeps the demand rising for land. As long as human nature doesn't change, people will always want more. When it comes to land, the supply can't be increased, so it's about as certain as anything can be that values will keep rising.

Plenty of Land, Plenty of Opportunity

Some real estate experts take the position that since land is not as scarce as many seem to think, and in fact exists in undeveloped abundance, it's unrealistic to expect the land boom to be sustained or prices inevitably to go up. These authorities point out that even though the use of land is increasing, there's still a lot left—more than will be needed in the next hundred years or perhaps ever. The fear of scarcity is an illusion, they say, caused by the population's crowding into metropolitan clusters that account for only a tiny fraction of the land. America has plenty of uninhabited, unused land and most of it won't experience any significant rise in value for a long time.

The point these experts miss is that plenty of land means plenty of opportunity for you and me to make big money for a long time. Sure there are still great gobs of undeveloped land in America, despite widespread suburban growth and the feverish development of vacation land, and a lot of it might not be a good investment for a while. But a lot of it is, too, and much of it can be bought in small pieces by individual investors in search of locations where land is likely to rise in value soon under the pressure of approaching demand.

The fact that the supply is still large doesn't change the fact that the supply never gets larger. The supply of land remains the same while demand increases with the population, the nation's affluence, and people's desire for more land. So the price of some land has to go up. All you need to do is learn how to tell which land that is.

Combating Inflation and Turning It into Profit

Investment in land is one of the best hedges against inflation that there is—quite possibly *the* best. You can lose on the stock market even during an economic boom or other period of rising prices. You can actually lose in what appears to be the safest of all investments—a government-insured bank savings account—during a period of inflation, if the inflation rate is higher than the interest rates paid on savings. In that circumstance, you do not get enough return on your invested capital to offset the loss in purchasing power through inflation. However, the effect of inflation on land is always to drive prices up, usually faster than the overall inflation rate.

A 1940 dollar was worth 36 cents in 1972, but the average real estate dollar appreciated to $3.60 during that same time. The general price level rose about 30 percent from 1960 to 1970, but land values increased 100 percent. Economists have predicted an inflation rate as high as 60 percent or higher over the 1970–80 decade, and events in 1974 indicated their estimates may have been too conservative. If land prices maintain the same relationship to the inflation rate as they did in the 1960's, that would mean an average increase of 200 percent in land values from 1970 to 1980.

This makes land a good retirement plan investment—better than a savings account, an annuity, or a pension program, where the value of your retirement dollar return is eroded by inflation. In land, the dollars invested gain in value along with inflation.

In addition, if you use time-payment financial leverage to spread your investment over a number of years on a land contract or purchase money mortgage, you keep investing cheaper dollars at the old price while your land appreciates in value.

When you buy on time, you are in effect borrowing the difference between your down payment and the purchase price—either from the seller or a third-party lender such as a bank. Borrowers always benefit from inflation because they repay their debts with cheaper money than they borrowed, since each dollar has lost purchasing power in the meantime. Borrowers also are able to recover some of their interest costs through their deductability on the federal income tax, where the effect is to reduce your tax bill.

When Prices Do Fall and How to Profit from That

Land prices usually do fall in a catastrophe like the Great Depression that plunged the world into misery during the 1930's. But that's about the only time, except when prices are higher than true value in the first place. When things are that bad, your investments are in big trouble no matter where you have your money. But you're still better off with land, since all you have to do is hold on to the land while you ride out the crisis. Your land isn't going to disappear. Corporations go bankrupt and governments disintegrate, but land remains. Novelist Anthony Trollope once said, "Land is about the only thing that can't fly away," and he was obviously right. It might be a strain to pay taxes or keep up the payments, and in fact many lost their land because they couldn't make those payments during the Great Depression. But, since everyone else is in the same economic depression, your chances are still better with land.

Such a circumstance, actually, can be a boon of opportunity to an alert investor in real estate. Since prices are down, it's a good time to buy. Land is more certain than practically anything else to resume rising in value when the economy recovers its equilibrium and energy. Many who got rich on land in the late 1940's and 1950's had acquired much of their holdings during the 1930's when sellers were extraordinarily desperate.

One of the favorite techniques was to buy property at sheriffs' tax sales, also called distress sales, where land was auctioned to pay delinquent taxes that hardpressed owners couldn't afford. Purchasers were able to acquire a great deal of valuable property for just the amount of the unpaid tax bills—often only a few dollars. The owners who lost land this way knew well enough it would someday recover its value and continue to rise in price, but they were powerless to avoid losing it. Property can still be bought at such tax sales, but very little is worth buying. In times of affluence, most defaults are by owners who can afford to pay the taxes, or who could sell their land easily enough, but who decide the property or the price they could get for it is not worth the taxes.

There are also times when land prices hold relatively steady for a while rather than climb. Or there may be particular local circumstances or factors that cause land prices to get stuck for a while, or even drop temporarily. But in most cases that means it's time to shop because it's easy to find a seller who's getting impatient or an otherwise good buy.

No Way to Lose if You're Careful

You will probably profit someday no matter what land you buy. No land is completely worthless and sooner or later it will be in demand. The difference is how long it takes. Even if you make a mistake and have to wait a while, or something unforeseen such as a depression intervenes, you still have the land.

You can plant vegetables on it and reduce your grocery expenses, put up a stand and sell ice cream bars, or just use it for picnicking, as our family did with our Kalkaska land during the four years we had it. I once owned another small piece of land for a while and a farmer paid me a few dollars a year to let him grow some crops on it. At the very least you can view it as a long-term investment that will provide for your retirement or your heirs.

If your land isn't increasing in value at the moment, it will someday. And it's always there. Land is the safest investment in the world, the closest there is to foolproof—as long as you're careful to avoid paying too high a price when you invest, to make sure the land is suitable for use, and, perhaps the most important secret of all in profiting on land, to buy in the right location.

3

THE SECRET OF
RICHES ON THE FRINGE

There's an old saying in real estate that goes something like this: "The three most important things in real estate are location, location and location."

That might be a slight exaggeration, but not much. Location is almost always the main determinant of the use to which land can be put, and use or potential use determines the value. The "higher," or more profitable or expensive, the use, the more valuable the land.

The most valuable land is generally that which is suitable for commercial purposes, since this type of use ordinarily produces the greatest profit per square foot of land. Location is practically always the key factor in determining whether a piece of land can be used legally and profitably for commercial enterprise. The condition of property can be altered; trees can be cut down and swampland can be filled in. The character of surrounding land can be modified to remove obstacles to a "higher" use. But it's not possible to change a property's location.

So, location is the No. 1 consideration in buying real estate for investment profit. This is true of all types of real estate, including improved property like houses, apartments, office buildings, stores, factories, shopping centers, restaurants and gas stations. In raw land, which is more certain than improved property to rise in value sooner or later, location is the prime factor in how soon it will rise.

The Basic Concept of the Fringe

The basic formula for success in buying raw land for appreciation profit was perhaps best articulated in a bit of succinct advice that's credited to John Jacob Astor. As the story goes, Astor once said, "Buy on the fringe and wait."

Astor had the resources to buy up huge tracts of land and wait long years until the American frontier expanded out to them, bringing development and price hikes. You can do the same kind of thing today on smaller frontiers with a lot less money, and, by applying a refined, more careful version of Astor's tactic, you can make your profits faster. The secret is to buy not only "on the fringe" of development, but in a precisely pinpointed location that offers the best chances for quick profit from early arrival of development activity.

It's this strategy that enables you to have both low risk and high profits. Ordinarily in investments, you must take greater risks in order to get an opportunity for bigger profits. If you prefer more certainty, more safety, and less risk, you usually must settle for less potential profit. As the world's safest investment, land would ordinarily be expected to produce modest returns. But strategic location on the fringe of development can mean big profits fast, too. The usual rule doesn't apply.

Buying a Jump Ahead of Development

The best place to look for quick profits in raw land is down the road from the current boom. Determine where development is barely beginning, where it's likely to go next, and where it probably will go after that. You don't follow the crowd; you get there a step or two ahead of it. You don't join the rush; you go around it and beat it to its next stop. You don't buy where development is already in full bloom; you stay a jump ahead and sell at a nice profit to the developer when he gets there.

There are some real estate experts who say that choosing land that can later be sold at a profit is just as chancy as picking a stock that will go up. But they're forgetting that there's a lot less danger that land values will go down and that it's much easier to predict the future of a piece of land from available facts. Development does sometimes hop around with unexpected choreography and fail to follow a logical pattern. But, for the most part, you can ascertain the direction of development with a high degree of accuracy. You don't need luck to do this, but careful study and evaluation. In any case, the risk is small. Even if you guess wrong, and the next expansion veers off in a surprise direction or does a leapfrog over your investment, the worst that can happen is that you'll have to wait longer to cash in.

Fringe Buying in Action

Before I purchased 80 acres near Kalkaska, Mich. a few years ago, I had been planning for several months to invest in northern Michigan land. I knew vaguely, from reading the newspapers and talking with my dad, who was then a part-time real estate salesman, that something of a boom had begun. Land in many areas was already expensive and I feared it was too late to get any sharp increases in value—though as it turned out later such land ballooned two and three times higher in price again within the next five years.

I began to look for less expensive acreage, though I didn't know exactly where to look. I had only a dim notion of the "fringe" concept at that time. I figured that if land in one area was once cheap and increased in value as more people built vacation cottages there, then there must be other places where land was still cheap but where people would be building many cottages a few years later as the vacation-land boom spread.

Though I had a vague idea that such land would have to be some distance away from developed areas where tourists and vacationers were already tripping over each other, I didn't know how far or in what direction to look, or how to recognize what I had in mind if I saw it. I could find low-priced land, but did not understand how to tell what areas were likely to be in the path of early development.

In the end, actually, I sort of lucked into a good fringe area without really knowing it. I looked casually through the want ads in the Detroit newspapers and took a few weekend drives up north with my wife and two daughters to scout around for "For Sale" signs. When I finally did find the 80 acres we bought, I was not at all sure it was the right thing and not very thorough about checking the area for clues about the nearness of development.

The owner was a leathery old codger named Kermit Riddle, who took us for a bumpy ride in a crumpled old Rambler over the lumber trails and through the trees on the land he had for sale. The terrain was what is described in advertising as "gently rolling" and the land was covered with handsome trees, including a lot of pine. Even in the dreary, wet cold of that October day, the bright fall colors of the maple tree leaves seemed bright and buoyant. The fresh aroma of pine was seductive. Thoroughly captivated, we almost bought on the spot.

But, we told Mr. Riddle that while we liked his land, we wanted to think it over, and drove into Kalkaska to inspect the town. We noticed no vacation home developments in the area and little new construction or commerce. The town, in fact, looked more like a ghost town than a vacation center. It seemed a pretty poor bet for an investment based on prospects for vacationland development in less than ten years.

A Lucky Stumble into a Smart Move

Our inspection of the area was far too casual and superficial. There were signs that development had taken root—for instance, a big development project getting started a few miles away—but I didn't see them. I failed to do the things you should do, such as talk to local businessmen, public officials and real estate agents, or drive all the nearby roads to see what growth could be detected. Our decision to buy two 40-acre parcels turned more on our unscientific liking for the land and conviction that it would increase in value someday, even if not soon, than on any careful assessment of facts and prospects bearing on how soon development could be expected to boost land values in that area. We were lucky that the venture turned out so well. It was the best use to which I ever put $200, the amount of my down payment. Four years later, I made $6,000 when I sold it and reinvested a good part of that in more land, which recently—only seven years after I bought the 80 acres near Kalkaska—was worth about $50,000.

Though I bought the Kalkaska property with the calculated expectation that vacationland development would sooner or later drive up its value, I was surprised that it happened so fast. I stumbled onto the Kalkaska scene at just the right time—just after development had begun but just before prices left the launching pad. I had acted on a good theory—buy land that's sure to be in demand later—but I was operating only halfway on sound methods.

I had only vaguely considered the matter of how long it would take for development and demand to hit the area with significant impact, which I later realized is a crucial question in effective investing for quick profit. In fact, I proceeded with the purchase even though I thought it might take a while. That I profited so quickly was largely a matter of luck.

Learning from Painless Mistakes

Information had been available that would have enabled me to decide almost entirely on facts instead of half on luck—information that developers were already moving into the Kalkaska area. The signs of approaching demand had been there. But I had not known enough to look carefully for them. What little checking I did was shamefully inadequate. I didn't even go to the county courthouse to check property and tax records for possible problems, or ask anyone if the land got swampy when it rained. Later I understood that to invest in land with so little information about it, and its surrounding area, is dangerous.

I learned from the experience, though, and it's much nicer to learn from experience while being lucky than from experience that's painful.

My Kalkaska experience taught me that some land increases faster than other land and the investor seeking short-range profit must make an effort to learn which land is most likely to appreciate rapidly—including such specifics as whether a piece of land is located on an improved road. I also learned that there are ways to get facts on whether an area is entering or about to enter a period of rapid development, how far off development is likely to be, what kind of development can be expected, and what direction it will take.

How to Start Looking

The land boom of recent years has been visible mostly in huge developments in Florida and Arizona with alluring names like Palm Coast and Rio Rancho Estates by such giant firms at ITT, AMREP, McCulloch, Boise Cascade, Horizon Corp., and Gulf American. But these do not represent the kind of land development that is useful to the average investor in search of profit on raw land, except as they may tend to drive up the values of surrounding land. Prices are already exorbitant in these developments. The profit is already used up.

Nevertheless, such developments can serve as a clue to areas on the fringe of development. The first thing you must do when you begin looking for land that's likely to be ripe for development soon is to determine where development is now underway, whether it's suburban land or vacation property. Then, moving out from there to areas where prices are lower and no apparent development has begun, you start looking for attractive parcels that are for sale. This can be done by scanning the want ads in newspapers, visiting a real estate office or two to see what's been listed with brokers, and driving the roads in search of "For Sale" signs.

At this point, you can also begin learning about an area you suspect may be in the path of development. This you can do by talking to real estate agents, reading the local newspapers carefully, and asking questions of local officials, businessmen, bankers, builders and developers. It's not necessary to make intensive efforts to gather information at this time, since you can wait until you locate a prospective piece of property before seeking details about any area, but it can help you narrow the area of search in the first place.

A Few Crucial Questions to Ask

Either way, you inquire about the area and its growth trends. Officials and staff members of planning commissions and zoning boards can be especially helpful if they are willing to talk to you. Real estate brokers who have been in business for several years are among the people who are most likely to be knowledgeable on the key points—namely, what direction growth in the area is expected to take; how fast it is expected to move; what kind of development is likely to be involved; what the plans of developers in the area are; where residential, commercial and industrial or recreational development is expected next and what is now on the planning board; who the people are that are most likely to know where future development will spread and what its nature will be; what land is most likely to be overtaken first by development; what land will probably be in demand for "higher" use; and where the developments are that are already under way and will affect land values. You put together what information you gather on these points and evaluate it to determine the best places to concentrate your search for a location where prices are low today but likely to start soaring tomorrow. Keep in mind that the closer you buy to existing developments at a low price, the better your chances for quick profit.

A big development project like Hidden Valley Lake in California might well be part of an overall vacation-land growth in its area that a small investor can turn to his advantage. If so, it's a clue to a place where you might start looking. But it's important to check further into the situation and not rely entirely on the existence of the project. Another Hidden Valley Lake, like the one in southern Indiana about 30 miles west of Cincinnati, O., may, on the other hand, be an isolated development that has little impact on surrounding property values. The only way to learn for sure is to investigate, yourself.

How to Locate Growing Areas

There are many developing areas, both suburban and vacation-land, where no big development project is underway, though smaller undertakings may be in evidence. You can find such areas easily enough by reading the real estate sections of daily newspapers, by talking to real estate agents, by asking others who have invested in land or own property in a resort area or suburb, by driving about in a car with your eyes open and your mind alert, by keeping a vigilant eye peeled while traveling and while on family outings, by reading brochures and advertising materials put out by chambers of commerce and real estate firms, and by talking to bankers, developers, and a community's political, civic and business leaders. These last may not tell you everything they know, but you can still learn a lot about the probable course and timetable of residential development, industrial expansion, shopping center locations and resort development. If you do not know such people and hesitate to approach them, you can best begin learning about developing areas and land that will next be ripe by going to a real estate broker as a prospective buyer and investor. Then go to a second, third and perhaps a fourth broker to get a balanced perspective, and to use what you learn from one to pry more information out of another.

What Vegas and Vermont Have in Common

Though there are generally two kinds of areas where continuing development keeps producing opportunities for profit in strategically located fringe land—suburban and vacation-land—there is one kind of land that more and more often is falling into both categories. This is farm land, which is getting an upward push on prices from both directions. Spreading metropolitan areas are soaking up farm land for residential subdivisions and shopping centers while at the same time "resort community" developers are buying up old farms for their projects. In some parts of the country the suburban boom is meeting head on with the paradise-in-the-country boom.

The newest wrinkle in big superdevelopments, in fact, is a combination of year-round residence and resort amenities in one place—a suburban home and vacation home all in one package. Developments like ITT's Palm Coast in Florida and McCulloch's Lake Havasu City and Fountain Hills in Arizona bill themselves as master-planned, "total environment" communities for permanent residence, four-seasons recreation, environmental Utopia, and gracious retirement living to boot.

New York, Pennsylvania, Vermont and other states have areas in demand both for exurban residences by big city executives and for mountain cabin sites by skiing enthusiasts. In the West, areas that a few years ago were barren desert outside Phoenix, Albuquerque and Las Vegas are now bustling suburbs or the sites of new "total community" development projects that promise year-round vacation style living amidst golf courses and lakes.

Completion of an interstate freeway into Vermont and the opening of Expo in Montreal sent land values skyrocketing from $100 an acre to $800 an acre, and in ski areas as high as $25,000 an acre, within a few short years. Lake Havasu City, the Arizona development which McCulloch Corp. calls America's first planned community and where the famous London Bridge was transplanted from England to help promote lot sales and make the development a tourist gimmick as well, is within commuting distance of Las Vegas and Phoenix. Other developments near Las Vegas trade on the area's attraction as a tourist mecca, its warm climate and its recreation opportunities to offer combined suburban-resort living.

The Secret of Imminent Use Change

There are hundreds of places in America where development is booming and land prices are rising. All you need to do in order to profit from this fact is to get out on the fringe of development in one of those places and buy land that's still low in price but soon to be overtaken by the demand of growth.

The kind of land you must seek is land that is about to undergo a usage change, or a change in anticipated or potential use. Land takes its biggest value leap when it moves from a state of non-use and low demand to a condition of desirability for an imminent or potentially profitable use—when it starts becoming noticeable to investors and speculators.

Land adjacent to developing land has already experienced that sharp rise in value. Its price has already gone up in anticipation of demand by developers and users. Land a bit farther away has already begun to rise in value, too, since its proximity to development has signaled a coming change from non-use to use. The land that offers you the best prospect for sharp increase is that which is located farther out, yet—on the fringe, where the change from non-use to use in the not-too-distant future is only beginning to be perceived.

A Matter of Sharp Timing

When unused raw land becomes recognized as feasible for development soon into vacation lots, suburban homesites, or an auto service station site, its value does a high-speed takeoff. As development draws near and it starts to become obvious that the land will soon be in demand, the price rise gathers momentum. The tactic that will make big profits fast is to get there and buy just before this sharp increase begins, or just after it begins and before it gains speed.

To spot such opportunities, you must assess the characteristics of an area and its growth patterns so that you can detect where potential use is about to change drastically, or has already begun to change, due to the spread of development. This means, for instance, finding out the anticipated direction of commercial expansion (shopping centers and stores) in a metropolitan area so that you can perceive when a piece of agricultural or residential land is well located and otherwise has good prospects for commercial use in the near future.

The tactic that must be learned thoroughly and kept constantly in mind is to buy land just as its value begins to increase in anticipation of a usage or demand change, hold onto it for two to five years as that anticipation grows in intensity, and then sell it at the higher price generated by the demand that the growing anticipation has produced.

The Profits and Politics in Rezoning

Though the best opportunities for big profits in a short time are to be found in low-priced raw land bought as it begins to be seen generally as having worthwhile use in the near future, good profits can also be made in land that already has risen a good distance in value but can yet zoom considerably higher because of usage-change possibilities. Land also shoots up in value when its potential use changes from one projected use to a more expensive, or more profitable, category. An example of this is residential land that has been intended for single-family dwellings, but suddenly is seen as more suitable for apartments. Since multiple-unit dwellings generally return a greater profit than single-family housing, both for landlords and developers, the land becomes more valuable when such a usage change becomes feasible.

This is why local zoning laws often attract corruption. While designed to give local governments control over land use and growth patterns, zoning laws also put into the hands of a few people—members of zoning appeal boards, planning commissions and town councils—an immense power to permit or deny huge profits to land investors and speculators.

When a man can sell a piece of land for $50,000 instead of $10,000 if he can get it rezoned for commercial use, he can often justify to himself improper means to bring it about, including the buying of influence or outright bribery. This situation submits local officials to severe temptation and pressure from those who pursue profits ruthlessly.

A small investor should understand how zoning works and how to go about getting a zoning change in a proper manner, since good opportunities often arise that are hard to seize unless you understand zoning. Some of the biggest profits are made by investors who get their land rezoned for "higher" use before they sell. Buying land that's already zoned for commercial or industrial use can be riskier than buying raw land for which no final zoning has been decided, because the sharpest price rises may already have taken place. But that's not always the case. Sometimes land can be bought for a relatively low price considering its prospects even though it's already zoned for an expensive use. Sometimes land is zoned for commercial use long before it's in much demand for that purpose, leaving the price low for future sharp appreciation. I once made the mistake of passing up commercial frontage selling for $100 a foot; five years later it was priced at $1,000 per foot.

However, it's not necessary to get involved in rezoning situations in order to make big money in land, especially in vacation-land areas that have not yet enacted or begun to enforce strict zoning laws or development restrictions.

Being Alert to the Next Disneyland

It's an advantage to have advance inside information about a coming event that will drive prices up, or access to private knowledge about the likely course of an area's growth. But it's not necessary. You can get enough information about the probabilities of an area's development to pinpoint good buys with a little routine investigation and study. You don't need to be privy to a lot of secrets or inside dope. You can even get an idea where a new shopping center will probably be located or how soon a big apartment complex will be built before everyone else reads it in the newspapers—just by beginning to look for good locations and talking to people who know. Actually, you can do well enough just by moving fast when a spectacular development affecting land prices becomes public.

The announcement that Disney World was to be built in Florida started prices in the area on a dizzy upward spiral that still hasn't ended. Disney Productions paid an average of $180 an acre and some land nearby shot up to $40,000 an acre afterwards. But it wasn't too late to buy on the fringe, and it still isn't. The price-boosting impact of Disney World on surrounding land will continue to ripple outward for many years. If you can't learn about such an occurrence in time to buy land cheap before public knowledge sends prices into orbit, the next best way to profit from it is to get out on the fringe quickly and buy land that's just beginning to go up in value because of it. It usually will join the skyrocketing soon.

Land in the area of the huge new Dallas-Fort Worth Airport in Texas zoomed in value from $1,000 an acre to $10,000 an acre in a five-year period after plans to build the airport were announced. Those who moved quickly after the announcement were able to buy while prices were still low and make hefty profits within a short time.

The main point to remember, though, is that you don't need to rely on that kind of special happening to make big money in land. There are plenty of places where development is spreading in less spectacular but nevertheless relentless fashion. All you need to do to find these places and pick out profitable fringe locations at low prices is to go look for them. Development is where you find it, and profit is on its fringe.

4

HOW TO FIND REAL ESTATE GOLD IN SUBURBIA

In less than 20 years, land outside cities like Albuquerque, N.M., Tuscon, Ariz., and Palmdale, Calif., increased in value from $15 an acre to $8,000 an acre and more. Land in what is now Scottsdale, a suburb of Phoenix, sold for $1 an acre just after World War II but recently it sold for more than $3,000 an acre.

Homer Hoyt, president of a Washington, D.C., real estate appraisal and analysis firm, told me that land values in Fairfax County, Va., jumped from $200 an acre to $12,000 an acre over a 20 year period. Land developed for shopping centers had risen to as much as $140,000 an acre, Hoyt said.

Thomas J. Purcell, president of Hogan and Farwell, Inc., a real estate appraisal company in Chicago, Ill., told me that land selling in Illinois for $500 to $700 an acre several years ago was going for $60,000 an acre recently. Property in Orange County, Calif., escalated in value from $3,000 an acre to $30,000 an acre in less than 10 years. Highway frontage that I could have bought north of Detroit, Mich., for $100 a foot a few years ago is now worth $1,000 a foot.

No End in Sight for Suburban Expansion

The days of such tremendous price rises in suburban land are by no means over. Though the exploding spread of suburbs has been going full blast now for a quarter of a century, it promises to continue, probably with even greater momentum, for many years to come. Suburbia keeps extending itself like an irresistible wave farther and farther out from hundreds of cities all over America. In fact, a strong case can be made for the proposition that we are actually still in the early stages of a suburban growth phenomenon that will span a century or two before it levels off.

Evidence that suburbia is growing faster than ever today can be found in the way that farmland prices keep rising at an ever-increasing rate. From November, 1969, to November, 1970, farmland prices increased an average of three percent in the United States, according to the U.S. Department of Agriculture. The following year, from November, 1970, to November, 1971, the increase was five percent. From March, 1971, to March, 1972, the increase soared to eight percent.

The main reason for this is that more and more farmland is being converted into residential subdivisions and shopping centers as metropolitan growth keeps spreading outward, both in the haphazard fashion it has followed to date and in the newer, more controlled developments that are coming into vogue. According to a 278-page report released near the end of 1974 by the U.S. Environmental Protection Agency, the U.S. Department of Housing and Urban Development and President Gerald Ford's Council on Environmental Quality, the unceasing growth of metropolitan areas was turning rural land into suburban property at the rate of 2,000 acres a day in the United States. Developers, meanwhile, generate further demand by use of the fringe buying concept for their own purposes. They often buy large tracts that look promising for future development.

From Cities to Supercities

As many experts predicted, the space between large cities like Washington and Baltimore or New York and Philadelphia, is filling up with houses, apartments, stores, office buildings, motels and factories, making huge supercities or megalopolitan complexes. As this happens, land values keep rising.

Land near a proposed New Town development north of Cincinnati, O., recently doubled in price within six months after the development was announced. "In 10 or 15 years, it will be all city from Dayton to Cincinnati," says Larry J. Fortman, head of Investors Companies Inc. of Columbus, O. "If I were you, I'd go down there and buy 100 acres near I-75."

There's almost certain to be growth around your city or one not far from you, even if there is no general boom. There are always metropolitan areas where some sections are growing fast, even during a nationwide economic recession. There's always some growth somewhere, and places where growth is about to begin. There are still hundreds of opportunities to make big money in raw land that's on the verge of being in demand for suburban growth. In fact, there are more such opportunities than ever, because there are more American cities with growing suburban areas than ever before.

Why the Suburban Boom Won't Stop

Suburban growth is fueled mostly by a relentlessly growing demand for more residential land and housing that shows no sign of abating—a demand that brings along a need for more commercial and other types of property as well. Even during a time of a construction industry slump (such as in 1973–74), there are still places where builders can't keep up with demand.

Despite the declining birth rate in America, the population will keep growing for at least 50 years. If the birth rate should rise again, so will the population growth. At the same time, the desire for better living also keeps growing. Everyone wants a nicer house and usually can find a way to get one. Millions of Americans already have fled the city and its ills to find a dream home on a green suburban plot of land, helped and encouraged by a booming economy, gains in personal affluence, and government-supported efforts to make mortgage financing easy to get. Millions more, still in the city, hope yet to escape urban poverty and inner-city troubles and join the middle class mainstream in the suburbs. Additional help and encouragement has been provided them by new laws and government programs to break down racial discrimination barriers and bring about equal opportunities for blacks and other minorities in education, jobs and housing. A start toward those goals has been made and one of the results of increased income among blacks has been their movement into suburban areas. It's only been a trickle so far, but when great numbers become able to afford the realization of the American dream home in suburbia, the new suburban growth explosion that results may make the 1950–70 flight to suburbia look like a study in slow motion.

Farther Out and Fancier Tastes

Increasing affluence, meanwhile, has heightened the desires and expectations of the veteran suburbanite. What ten years ago was a peaceful, spacious homesite in a pleasant suburb now seems too small, too old, too much like the city, and not nice enough for his improved economic standing. So he moves further out to a newer suburb, doing his part to keep suburbia growing, in his yearning for a bigger, more expensive home and handsomer, more spacious grounds. In some areas, this trend has extended suburbia so far out from the city's core that it's called exurbia, and sleepy rural towns have been transformed into extravagant bedroom suburbs with soaring land prices.

Young adults starting new families today also have fancier tastes in housing, and more exalted notions of what's ordinary than their parents had, due to the affluence of the times. Twenty years ago, newlyweds figured they'd be lucky if they could afford a home of their own within ten or 20 years. Now they consider it normal to buy a spiffy new home right after the honeymoon, or even before the wedding. They see no compelling reason to scrimp on price, either, since they can pay for it from future income.

How Suburban Growth Picks Up Momentum

Not only is the demand for residential land growing, but the character of the demand is changing, too. Not only are there more people wanting land, but people also think they need more land. And events keep making it easier to satisfy their wants. The building of multi-lane, limited access freeways radiating out into the country from cities has enabled Americans to move farther and farther out and still drive to work. Factories, office buildings and jobs have joined the move of people and stores to the suburbs, too, permitting workers to move even farther away without inconvenience.

This has set in motion what cities see as a vicious circle. As business and industry leave the city to catch up with the people who already have fled to suburbia, the city suffers a loss in tax revenue and a further loss in incentive for residents to remain in the city. Attempting to recoup the tax losses, many cities have passed an income tax, which in turn has driven still more residents to the suburbs. Some cities have tried to stop this by taxing the income of suburbanites who work in the city, but that also has produced the unwanted boomerang effect of putting another pressure on employers to move to the suburbs—so their employees can escape the tax.

What all this means is that suburban growth is sure to continue for a long time, and to make available many opportunities for big profits in raw land. All you need to do is buy some strategically located land a bit before the growth gets to it.

An Example of How to Profit on the Suburban Fringe

My first real estate investment, even before I bought my first home, was an attempt to profit from the suburban growth situation when much of the area north of Detroit was developing fast. I began looking in Troy, then being touted as the next boom suburb in the Detroit area, where I had lived most of my life. Prices of land in Troy seemed already high. As it turned out a few years later, they were actually still quite low. Any land in that area would have brought a big profit in a few years. But at the time the prices seemed too high, so I looked farther out.

Driving along a state highway, M-150, north of Troy, I found a "For Sale" sign near a spot where a new highway was to cross M-150 and a new interchange was to be built. Checking further with the state highway department and township officials, I discovered that this land would be right next to the interchange—a perfect location for a gasoline station. Service station sites command as high a price as any land in a growing suburb, perhaps the highest, since they are always in prime commercial locations—on a corner or next to a freeway ramp—and the oil companies pay top dollar. The going price for gas station sites in that area then was about $40,000 and would no doubt be much higher next to an interchange, especially by the time it finally got built.

The price of the parcel was $9,000. It was only 1.7 acres in size, but it had 225 feet of frontage on M-150 and was plenty big enough for a service station. Its location on the highway near an interchange meant that eventual commercial use of some type was inevitable, even though the land was then zoned agricultural. It seemed an obviously shrewd investment—not speculation at all—and I scraped up the $1,000 down payment I needed to buy the land on a land contract.

A Fine Result Despite Some Bad Luck

My plan went a bit awry because the highway department's engineers moved the interchange 300 feet to the north and the state condemned most of the parcel, including all the frontage on M-150. Instead of sweet reveries about a big bundle from an oil company, I had a big fight with the State of Michigan, which offered me only $9,000 for the land—the same price I had paid for it—even though it was three years later and land prices in the area had gone up despite the failure of the expected boom to materialize in Troy. I found prices along M-150 in the area ranging from $55 a front foot to $278 a foot, which Sun Oil Co. was offering for a nearby parcel. $9,000 for my land represented only $40 a foot.

I made some profit, however, when the condemnation jury awarded me $11,000 (about $49 a foot) and I had $1,334 left after paying my attorney. That wasn't too bad for the amount I had invested during the three years I had owned the land, but the best part is that I still have .7 acre left that the state didn't take. Though there's no access to the land because the state took all the M-150 frontage, the remaining piece is now zoned for commercial use, adjoins the site where the service station did go, and is valued for tax purposes at $6,300.

The lack of access is a tricky, but not insurmountable problem. It can be solved by completing a short distance of a subdivision street to the back of the property. Business land in that area was recently appraised at $2 to $2.50 a square foot, and in prime locations as much as $3 a square foot, as development in the area finally got into gear after the highway was completed in 1973. This was before it was announced that a giant new shopping mall was to be built half a mile north. At just the low figure of $2 a square foot, the 30,000 square feet I still own is worth $60,000—and going up. And I have no investment in it at all, since I got more from the state than I originally paid for the entire parcel. All it costs me to wait for the right time to cash in is $160 a year in taxes.

My big mistake was not buying more land in that area a few years ago even if I had had to borrow money to do it. I could have bought land along M-150 for $100 a foot, some of it already zoned commercial and some of it across the street from the place where the new shopping mall is being built now. There was even some available for as low as $55 a foot. It was up to $1,000 a foot even before the shopping mall was announced. Several miles north, land that could have been bought for $200 or $300 an acre was recently on the market for $2,000 an acre and up.

Both in what I did do and in how I failed to seize obvious opportunities, you can see some of the techniques for seeking out land that's in the path of development and on the brink of a sudden value rise because of suburban expansion.

How to Spot Opportunities and Where to Look

One thing I should have done, for instance, was to have perceived more clearly the obvious conclusion to be drawn from the building of the new highway. I might indeed have acted to buy more land in that area if I had been more alert to what that meant.

Public knowledge of the highway plans had lifted land prices a little, but the major part of the impact was still in the future. I should have realized more precisely that land prices there would take another jump after highway construction began and the increases would gain momentum as it neared completion and attracted development. I knew that construction of a new highway is an event that drives up land values, but I managed to overlook the fact that this impact lasts over a period of years and is not exhausted overnight. It just didn't hit home that I should have bought more land there because it was sure to appreciate rapidly during the next few years as the highway was built.

This is an example of an opportunity that's available to everyone, including you. Many such events are going on in growing suburbs across the country and it's easy enough to know about them and take advantage of them to make money in land before their value-boosting impact runs out. Though you can do better if you have advance inside information, you can still make big profits without it. The first price jump is only a small part of the effect that such a development has on surrounding land values. The entire impact takes years to exert itself.

Making Use of Long Range Impact

If you act with dispatch after such a coming development becomes known, you still have time to buy a well-situated piece of land early in the value-increase period and profit when its value rises as the project materializes. This is true not only of a new highway, but also of other projects that drive up land prices, like a new shopping center, a housing development, or that modern new approach to controlled growth, the New Town or Planned Unit Development (PUD), in which an entire new community is constructed, complete with stores, office buildings, industrial zones, school and parks as well as apartments and houses. There's plenty of time to go out and buy land in the path of the development that follows in the wake of such projects. Prices will keep rising for years afterward, spurting when construction begins and again when it's completed, in an ever-widening circle.

You can also profit from the impact of smaller development projects that get less publicity, but which nevertheless increase land values in the area—such as a residential subdivision, an apartment complex or a new motel. Even road widenings increase land values. If you move quickly when it becomes known that new construction will take place, you can buy before the price rise gets a full head of steam, then profit as it does. You can do even better with less risk, of course, if you can learn about an area's development plans and trends ahead of the general public, whether any spectacular projects are involved or not. This is not hard to do, either.

Getting the Key Facts

Pinpointing the areas where the next suburban boom will hit, where new big projects will be located, or just where unspectacular development will spread, is not a matter for wild guessing, snap judgment or just surface observation. The difference between speculating and investing when it comes to land is getting the facts needed for accurate analysis, reliable prediction and intelligent decision.

There's no way to be totally scientific or 100 percent certain, but you can come closer to it in raw land than in any other type of investment that offers potentially big profits. This is because you have it within your power to get a great deal of information about an area's growth patterns and plans, and how they affect the land that you may consider buying. This enables you to minimize the element of chance and maximize the influence of prudence and astuteness. And it is easier than ever today to get the information you need, because local governments and private firms are doing more long-range planning on growth and development than ever before.

Most communities and counties in metropolitan areas have some system for planning and controlling their growth. Many have banded together to form multi-government planning commissions or regional planning agencies. These commissions and agencies conduct studies, prepare reports and draw up master plans showing where various types of development are expected to take place, and where they will be permitted. Such documents are usually matters of public record and are available for inspection by anyone who asks to see them. You need only find out from your city or town hall where such offices and records are located.

Records, Meetings and Members of Local Agencies

Ordinarily, you will also be able to find an official or employee at such an agency who is willing to fill in details for you and bring you up to date on changes since the last report or map was prepared. You can also attend public meetings of such planning bodies to hear for yourself some of the latest information about an area's development, or check to see how thoroughly the local newspapers report on their meetings.

Even smaller cities without sophisticated planning systems attempt some measure of growth control with zoning ordinances. Cities and counties with planning agencies also have a zoning system usually administered by separate boards. Local commissions and boards that decide and enforce zoning also hold public meetings, and their records and maps are open to the public.

There is usually much inside information that the members of such local government boards and planning commissions discuss only in private until they feel the time is appropriate for the public to know, but you can still learn a lot of basic information from this source. It provides you with a foundation of knowledge that better equips you to draw some of that inside information out of local officials, real estate agents, developers and others who have access to it. It also affords you a good general grasp of development opportunities for an area's raw land.

Specifics may well be obtainable—more so than ever before, in fact—from the growing number of real estate appraisal and analysis firms, real estate and development consultants, and investment counseling companies that have up-to-date data on development plans and trends. The goal here is to get access to their knowledge at minimum cost, such as by seeking a land investment through a real estate broker connected with such a firm or one that regularly uses the services of such a firm.

Narrowing Your Search

It's important to get a basic understanding of an area's development situation before you buy land, but you need to do it only once for each area. Then, as long as you can find enough good investments in the same general area, you can concentrate your efforts on evaluating specific pieces of land within the framework of the knowledge you already possess. In a large metropolitan area, there may be several sub-areas that you can focus on separately, especially since you may need to go out 40 to 60 miles to find a fringe area where prices are still low. Concentrating on the growth in just one direction can be enough to turn up many good fringe investment opportunities in such a circumstance. If you are dealing with a smaller urban area, say a core city of 100,000 to 200,000 population, you probably can find good investments only 10 to 15 miles from the center of town, or even fewer, and can get a firm grip on the entire area's development with ease.

Once you are grounded in the basics and set out to learn specifics by starting to prospect for good buys, you will discover it's quite easy to find out a lot about what's going on. Though you may well never know as much as the local real estate businessmen, developers, longtime investors and others in the business and real estate establishment, you will learn enough to make lots of money, and that's the main thing.

It's possible, for instance, to discover when a developer is trying to "package"—buy up or get options on—several small parcels for a big project like a shopping center, and to do it secretly so the prices won't leap up. Word does get around, however, especially among real estate agents, some of whom don't feel compelled to be quite so secretive about such things. You might well learn about it if you are aggressively looking for a good investment, digging out information about an area, and talking frequently with real estate agents whose brains you are trying to pick for all the information you can get. Most people who hear about such things remark on them to others, but seldom act on the opportunity to take advantage of the situation by purchasing for re-sale at a higher price to the packager, or profiting later from the price rise produced by the announcement of the project. One of the secrets of making money in land is to act when you discover opportunity.

Main Sources of Suburban Growth Data

Here is a summary of the main sources of information on a suburban area's growth and development:

1. Real estate agents.
2. Local government, especially planning commissions and zoning boards.
3. State commerce departments and other agencies dealing with development and land use.
4. Real estate consultant and investment counseling firms; real estate organizations and publications.
5. Developers, builders, their organizations and their publications.
6. Newspapers, magazines and other publications available at the public library or in the lobbies of real estate and development company offices.
7. Mortgage companies and banks.
8. Business leaders and chambers of commerce.
9. Operators of businesses in growing areas.

10. Real estate and development departments of major retail stores and franchise chains.

11. Investors and businessmen who have invested in land in the area and who are still active in the market.

12. Personal inspection.

The Importance of Timely Action

When you learn about the imminence of a new shopping center or become able to determine where development is sure to spread next, that's no time to hesitate. That's the time to act—to get out and start looking in earnest for a piece of good, well-situated land that's certain to have its value doubled or tripled within a few years as the inevitability of development in the near future becomes widely known, as projects are announced, and as construction begins and is completed. Never move too fast, impatiently or hastily; move carefully, with deliberation, and wisely. But the important thing is to move.

I, and some others, missed out on big profits in another area north of Detroit during the 1960's because we failed to act on our knowledge. We knew that the southeast part of Troy was an ideal and logical location for a major new shopping center to serve the many fast-growing suburbs north and northeast of Detroit. We thought it would be astute to buy some land in that area. Yet we never got around to it.

So we never made a cent when it was announced that a $15 million dollar shopping center was to be built on 128 acres located almost exactly where we had guessed. Then we made our next mistake; we still didn't buy. Prices took a big jump with the announcement, but then leveled off a bit. We figured it was still time to buy nearby land that would rise sharply in value as the shopping center neared reality. But we never got around to that, either.

So we didn't make any of the big profits that many others realized when that shopping center—Oakland Mall, one of the Midwest's biggest and busiest—opened up a few years ago. Nor did we profit from the rapid spread of development outward from the mall as land where farmers had been growing crops a few years earlier suddenly became the booming suburb that Troy had long promised to be. Development and rising land prices continue to ripple out even today, and no doubt will continue for years to come. There's still plenty of opportunity for one who acts on it.

Three Who Did Act and Reaped the Rewards

Three corporation executives in Dayton, O., who did act on their perceptions in a similar circumstance ended up with big profits. They saw how the suburbs south of town were growing fast early in the 1960's and began buying up land in the vicinity of a corner that appeared to be an ideal location for a shopping mall. After a while, the three men began contacting developers and department store executives to sell them on their location.

They eventually bought up nearly 400 acres and succeeded in selling the idea of building a shopping mall there. On that location today is the Dayton Mall, the largest, most modern shopping mall in Ohio's Miami Valley. It certainly wasn't luck. The three executives knew what the opportunity was and were enterprising enough to act on it. They also knew that even if they couldn't sell their land for a shopping center, it would still rise considerably in value as suburbia grew.

New Opportunities Down the Road

But they by no means exhausted the opportunities to make lots of money in land from the impact of the Dayton Mall. The ramifications continue today and, like the Oakland Mall north of Detroit, will keep raising land values over an ever-widening area for years to come. The opening of the Dayton Mall in 1970 touched off a development boom and land rush for miles in several directions, particularly along the main roads. A new shopping center not only *results* from suburban growth—it in turn *stimulates* more growth. In recent years, the area around the Dayton Mall was called "the hottest area in the country." New construction kept popping up and so did signs saying, "Possible Business Site, Will Build to Suit."

That boom is not only still going strong today but is burgeoning more feverishly than ever. It seems there are constantly more new gas stations, restaurants, stores, small shopping centers, drive-in theaters, bank branches, real estate offices, dental offices, muffler shops, golf driving ranges, discount stores, car washes, party stores, supermarkets, drug stores, shoe stores, medical clinics, barber shops, laundromats, apartment complexes, automobile dealerships, residential subdivisions, churches, motels and fast-food outlets. It's no longer a good time to buy there. But it is a good time to buy down the road a bit, where all this booming growth is headed.

What to Look For

After you've picked out a likely area on the fringe of active development, gathered information about the area's growth trends and expectations, armed yourself with guidance on how to look for a good investment, decided to act with all deliberate speed, and are ready to go looking for a good buy, all you need to know further is what kind of land to look for. It's important to remember that just buying on the fringe, while it may turn out all right, is riskier and not usually as profitable as finding the best spots on the fringe, the land that's especially likely to be in demand for high-return use because of its location and individual characteristics.

Here is a list of the best bets for quick, big profit—land that's most likely to appreciate in value sharply within a comparatively short time like two to five years if development is approaching:

1. Commercial Corners

Land with commercial use prospects has the highest potential value. Accurately ascertaining which low-priced land has the best potential for commercial use in the near future is the straightest path to big profits from suburban growth. The most valuable land of all is a commercial corner on two main roads, or at a freeway interchange. Such corners are in high demand by oil companies for auto service stations and by other business as well. It's almost impossible not to make a sizeable profit in such land, especially if it's already been zoned for commercial use so far in advance of actual commercial use or demand that its price is still low. For instance, if you can buy for $10,000 or less an acre of land on a main-road corner in an area likely to experience intensive development within five to 10 years, grab it.

2. Commercial Road Frontage

The next best bet is frontage on a main road near a commercial corner, near a new shopping center or other new construction, on a side-street corner, or an area otherwise likely to be in demand for commercial use within the next few years, whether already zoned for business use or not. Offering special potential in recent years and no doubt for many years to come is land that's suitable for one of the restaurants or fast-food outlets operated by America's proliferating franchise merchandising industry. The fantastic growth of such chains, from Kentucky Fried Chicken and Howard Johnson restaurants to McDonald's Hamburgers and Ponderosa Steak Houses, has generated a particularly intense demand for strategic sites in growth areas. You can learn the sizes and other specifications for such locations from real estate agents or by writing the real estate or development divisions of these franchise businesses at their home offices. I learned by writing to Mr. Steak Inc. that one of that firm's restaurants needs 30,000 to 33,000 square feet on a major thoroughfare with a high volume of traffic near a good commercial and industrial area, preferably near a shopping center, backed up by a dense residential area of single family and multiple dwellings with a minimum population of 75,000 in the market area. Denny's Inc. needs 40,000 square feet and 165 feet of frontage for one of its restaurants. Larger parcels may be suitable for discount stores or small shopping centers.

3. Office Building Sites

Many growing suburbs use their zoning regulations to restrict development in some sections to office use, including medical and dental offices as well as a wide variety of business offices. Land of various sizes and shapes may be suitable for this kind of use, and its value is almost as high as land that can be used for any kind of commercial purpose.

4. Industrial Land

Sites zoned for manufacturing and other industrial operations comprise the next most valuable type of land. Location on a main road is not as important as it is for retail businesses, but convenient access to freeways, railroads and/or an airport often is. Land not yet zoned for industrial use but situated where that use is most likely to be developed can be a good investment, especially if such development promises to take place soon.

5. Apartments

Land of both small and big size that would be feasible and attractive for development of multiple dwelling projects in the near future is often a wise investment, especially in areas where the suburban apartment lifestyle is just beginning to catch on. Federal tax laws have made apartment construction attractive to investors in search of depreciation tax shelters, and this has increased the demand for suitable land. Recent slumps in the construction industry have slowed down apartment construction, but when it revives again the rejuvenated demand will drive prices up again. Such land offers good investment prospects for the next several years.

6. Residential Land

Though land destined for development of single family homes rises in value along with other land, it does not increase as fast or go as high. The best way to obtain satisfying profits in this type of land is to buy large tracts at low prices well in advance of development.

Where the Lowest Prices Have Gone

The trickiest part of strategic fringe buying to profit from suburban growth is in locating land that has both:

1. Good prospects for sharp value rises within two to five years; and
2. Still a low price.

In these days of inflation, land close enough to existing development to have clearly good prospects is already expensive. I recently checked into a six-acre parcel with 400 feet of main road frontage in a fast-growing area northwest of Dayton, near my home. It is undoubtedly a good investment, since it's sure to be in demand for commercial use or apartments within a few years, but the price is already up to $35,000.

It's smarter to go out a bit farther for a lower price, or scout around for a parcel closer in whose prospects have somehow been overlooked by others. You can still find good buys that you can make with only a few hundred or few thousand dollars down if you look with determination. But the opportunities for big profits on small investments today are more plentiful and easier to find on the fringe of vacation-land development.

5

BIG PROFITS
IN VACATION LAND

Despite the continued expansion of suburbia at an ever-increasing speed in metropolitan areas across the nation, that's not where America's biggest land boom is. The scene of the main action in fast-rising land values is vacation land—land in growing demand for resort, recreation or retirement use in the woods and mountains, and on the lakes and seashores, of America.

Land prices in northern Michigan's rich vacation territory, for instance, have soared deliriously in recent years and are expected to keep right on spiraling dizzily into the stratosphere for many years to come. Freeways and resort towns are jammed with tourists and vacationers every weekend during the summer, the fall hunting seasons, and winter skiing and snowmobiling times. More and more of them are buying land so they'll have a place of their own for swimming, fishing, hunting and winter sports. One development company executive said, "All you have to do is get on the freeway on a weekend and see how good the market is."

Land in the Kalkaska area that I sold for $137.50 an acre in 1971 was up to $600 and even $1,000 for choice locations by 1974. Lake frontage in the Cheboygan area tripled in price within five years. On one small lake, 10-acre parcels that were priced from $5,000 to $8,000 were on the market a year later for $7,500 to $9,000. I recently could have bought 200 acres in Michigan's Upper Peninsula for $14,000, but the seller and I could not agree on a down payment. Sixteen months later, the price was up to $24,000.

Booms and Opportunities Across the Nation

Similar booms are going full blast in many other states, too, without sign of stopping. You can find rising land values just about any place where there are woods, mountains, lakes or seashore. You can also find them in such unlikely places as the deserts of Nevada and Arizona and the plains of western Ohio, where developers are constructing artificial lakes and slicing up the land around them.

The mountainous resort area of southern Tennessee and northwestern North Carolina is another fast-growing area for recreation, vacations and tourists. Gatlinburg, Tenn., just north of the Great Smoky Mountains, is one of America's gaudiest and busiest resort towns, perhaps second only to Las Vegas, Nev. Beech Mountain in North Carolina is the site of a flamboyant mountaintop amusement park based on the characters in "The Wizard of Oz" and a giant, 7,200-acre development project of vacation homes and condominiums. Other tourist attractions also abound in the mountains, and it's all producing a sizzling land boom. According to W. C. Johnson, a real estate broker in Asheville, N.C., wooded mountain land that sold for $30 to $80 an acre in 1960 was recently selling for more than $500 an acre.

And so it is across the nation, from Maine to Vermont to Arizona and California, from Florida to Montana, from Texas to Michigan. 200 acres in Washoe County, Nev., was advertised at $265 an acre in September, 1973. Two months later, the same property was advertised at $295 an acre.

Low Prices, Easy Starts, and Places to Look

What makes the vacation-land rush more of a potential profit bonanza than suburban growth, especially to the small investor, is plenty of low prices. If you don't have much money to work with, vacation land is an easier way to start. In fact, it's the easiest way there is to begin an investment program that gives you both low risk and high profits. When prices are low, so are down payments.

Good land can still be bought in Michigan's Upper Peninsula for $25 an acre. That means you can buy 100 acres for only $2,500—possibly for as little as $500 down. If you have no cash at all, you should be able to borrow that much. You should double your money in two or three years with no trouble at all.

Inexpensive land not only can be found on the fringes of areas already undergoing development, it can also be bought in relatively unpopulated areas in northeastern Vermont, Alabama, Oklahoma, Missouri, Nevada, Wyoming, Idaho, Montana, Kansas, Alaska and several Canadian provinces. Much of this land might not produce a profit for several years, but some of it will come into demand soon. The trick is to figure out which.

One of the hottest spots in recent years, though it has received little publicity about it, is West Virginia. A well-to-do young lawyer in that state, while handling estates, found a demand blossoming for farm properties among government officials and business executives in Washington, D.C., Baltimore and Virginia cities. It's becoming fashionable to buy up an old farm as a not-too-distant second home in the country.

The Benefits of Low-Price Leverage

A price of $25 an acre means the land doesn't have to appreciate very much for you to make a nice profit. When $25 land increases by $25 an acre, you double your money. If you pay $100 an acre, you make only 25 percent when it goes up $25. If you pay $250 an acre, you make a mere 10 percent. In the first case, you invest only $25 to make $25. In the second case, it takes $100, and in the third case, $250.

If you have only $2,500 to invest, you can buy 100 acres at $25 an acre and make $2,500 if it goes up $25. You can buy only 25 acres of $100 land, and you make only $625 when it goes up $25. If you pay $250 an acre, you can buy only 10 acres and make only $250. A price of $250 an acre is low enough for you to make a good profit where prices are likely to keep climbing, but it's easier to make big money at lower prices. The leverage of mathematics produces more result for the money input, just as the leverage of a crowbar produces more result for the energy input. Whatever you have to invest—$1,000 or $100,000—you make money faster in lower-priced land.

The lower the price, the greater the leverage. If you can buy land for $1 an acre, it needs to increase only $1 to double your money. When it goes to $10, you make 900 percent. $1 land is riskier, however; it's so remote that it may take quite a while to rise in value at all.

Low Down Payments That Disguise High Prices

Though low prices usually mean low down payments, too, low down payments don't always mean low prices. Many developers in Michigan, for instance, sell 10-acre parcels for $100 down, but the total price runs as high as $1,000 an acre. Lots in vacation-land development projects can be bought for as little as $5 down and $5 a month even though they're outrageously overpriced. Developed vacation land is almost always not as good an investment as undeveloped land. This is especially true in most vacation-land development projects.

Developers must recover their expenses, including enormous amounts for advertising and promotion, and make a profit, too. Land in development projects usually sells for at least 10 times more than the price the developer paid—meaning there's no profit left for you. It's not the plan that you be the exploitee. You should buy the land before the developer gets there, and perhaps sell to him when he does arrive.

In Michigan's Upper Peninsula a few years ago, people were buying 10-acre parcels in an extravagantly promoted project for $795 down. But the total price was $7,995, which was $799.50 an acre. Land in the area outside the project, where buyers weren't bothering to check, could be bought for only $70 an acre. A lot in a Pocono Mountain development project in Pennsylvania recently sold for $1,600 down. The total price, however, was $8,000, and since the lot contained only 12,364 square feet (about the same as a city lot), that figured out to $28,183 an acre. It's conceivable the price will go even higher someday, but the buyer would have better odds on making money with his $1,600 by purchasing lottery tickets.

Many development projects, including some by big development corporations as well as fly-by-night hustlers, use the practice of diverting a buyer's attention from total price by stressing low down payments and easy monthly payments—"your cost per month." Credit buying has unquestionably been a key force behind American prosperity in recent years, and now its widespread use in the selling of land development lots is one of the main ingredients in the vacation-land boom. You can make good use of installment buying, yourself, in your land investments. But be careful not to buy land with low payments that disguise high prices. The down payment is important as to how easy it is to buy, but the price is the key factor in the size of profits.

How to Start Looking

Though it's unwise to buy a lot in a development project, such projects represent the most visible manifestation of America's vacation and recreation land boom. They account for most of the estimated $6 billion a year being spent on such land by Americans. Hundreds of them, of all sizes, have sprung up across the nation in recent years. The best known and biggest are in Florida and Arizona, but many other states have lots of them, too. Some states, such as California, Colorado, Arizona and Michigan, have so many that they're rushing in alarm to install more controls on land development for protection of the environment. There are more than a hundred such projects in Michigan alone, with plots ranging from tiny lots to 10.1-acre parcels that avoid state subdivision controls. A Michigan official has stated that developers are selling more than 30,000 lots a year in that state's northern vacation land.

These projects, however, can serve as a clue to the location of development and rising land prices that are spreading out with opportunities on their fringes—though exploiting this ripple effect must be done with great care, since some projects are premature, overambitious, poorly located, or isolated from true demand or growth patterns. There are also plenty of other growing vacation-land areas across the country that afford opportunities to make money on the fringe. What you must do first to take advantage of these opportunities is to start looking for them.

There are hundreds of real estate firms in every state that have listings of vacation land or country properties for sale. Many of them put out lists, catalogs or brochures describing land parcels of all kinds and sizes, from lake lots and river cabin sites to large tracts containing several square miles, including improved and developed properties already containing a structure. To start finding out what's available, you need only contact realty firms, read the newspaper want ads under such headings as "resort property" and "acreage," and go out prospecting in your car.

You can pick an already developing area and move out a few miles from there, contacting realty firms in that area. You can write or call real estate agents in several likely areas. Or, you can check the newspapers and telephone directory *Yellow Pages* of cities within 500 miles of likely areas for the names of real estate firms to ask for catalogs or listings.

Some realty firms specialize in vacation land and their names can be learned from *Yellow Pages* advertisements, the local Board of Realtors or the nearest real estate agency. Telephone directories of other cities can usually be found at the public library. Libraries also have newspaper directories with the names and addresses of newspapers throughout the United States.

There are a few realty firms that operate nationally, often through a franchise arrangement or just a cooperative advertising setup among independent agencies. Others do likewise on a regional or statewide basis. One example is United Farm Agency, which publishes a national catalog of farm, country and vacation properties. You can probably find an affiliated agency through a real estate board, and get a catalog just by asking for one.

Some national publications carry real estate ads. At least one monthly paper, called *The Link,* contains nothing but real estate advertising. Its address is P.O. Box 48, Danville, Wa. 99121. Information on U.S. government land to be sold at auction can be obtained from the Bureau of Land Management in Washington. The government recently sold 1,700 acres in Arizona and California for an average price of $75 an acre, and 9,000 acres in Nevada for an average of $37 an acre.

An Example of How to Prospect for a Fringe Investment

After I sold my 80 acres in my fringe-investment venture near Kalkaska, I wanted to reinvest my profit on another fringe. I decided to combine my prospecting for a new investment with a family vacation tour of Michigan's Upper Peninsula, where I had learned one could still find plenty of good land at low prices.

I obtained information about several promising parcels from real estate firms and newspaper ads. As we mapped out our trip, we scheduled visits to these locations amongst the sightseeing excursions and tourist traps on our travels. A dash of business didn't detract at all from our pleasure. In fact, tromping around on vacation land for sale was as much fun, if not more, as riding through the Soo Locks or walking through an old copper mine.

We looked at several parcels of various sizes in different locations, including that 200 acres I should have bought for $14,000. But we didn't buy any of them. The best deal of all was one we came upon by accident one day while exploring the woods on a gravel road a few miles from Tahquamenon Falls. We came upon a lake and a "For Sale" sign tacked to a tree. We copied down an address and, after returning home from the trip, we sent a letter of inquiry.

We drove up there again in October to look at an 18-acre parcel near the lake and other land the owner had on the market, including several hundred feet on the undeveloped east shore of the lake, which was called Pike Lake. Pike Lake was barely big enough to be on the official state map, but its clear water sparkled and the bottom was all sand. There was development only on the north side. As we sauntered through the magnificent forest on the east shore, remarking how unspoiled and fresh the land felt, we fell in love again. We bought 600 feet of frontage on the lake.

Converting $200 into $50,000 in Seven Years on the Side

The owner was asking $50 a foot for the lake frontage, but agreed to accept $20,000 if I bought 600 feet. This figured out to $33.33 a foot. Compared to prices of other lake frontage I had checked, that was a good price, even though the area was comparatively remote and there were no signs that intense development could be expected soon. However, I did make more effort to learn about the area's prospects than I had with the Kalkaska land. I found that while extensive development was probably not near, there was talk about an increasing shortage in good lake frontage land.

I paid $2,500 down on a land contract and committed myself to payments of $120 a month. The transaction was finally completed, after exchanges of correspondence and documents through the mail.

Two years later, that lake property was appraised at $65 to $75 a foot. I put it on the market for $50,000—$83.33 a foot. If I sold it for $70 a foot, I would more than double my money—that is, even if I had paid the purchase price in full instead of buying on a time-payment arrangement.

Or, I could sell half of it, say with $4,000 or $5,000 down and monthly payments of $150 a month on a land contract. Besides making a profit on the 300 feet I sold, I'd have $4,000 to $5,000 to invest in more land, a monthly income of $150 that would more than cover my own payments of $120, and 300 feet of land remaining without further monthly investment from my own funds. This I could sell later at an even higher price.

All this began with the $200 down payment I put on 80 acres near Kalkaska. If I had put that $200 instead into General Motors stock, it would have been worth only about $120 seven years later. Also, if I had less than $2,500 to put down on the Pike Lake frontage, I could still have bought 100 feet or 200 feet without much cash. Even at $50 a foot, there was plenty of profit to be made in only two or three years.

And that's not all. From the same owner I also bought 600 feet of frontage on the gravel road, the main county road in that area, across from the entrance to the road that leads to the east shore of the lake. This parcel will take longer to bring me a good profit, but the profit will be huge when it does come. This land should be ideal for commercial development in a few years when development finally does reach Pike Lake in a big way. I paid only $2,000 for it—$500 down and $20 a month.

Getting the Key Facts

The sources of information on a vacation area's development potential are for the most part the same as those for suburban areas. Real estate agencies and developers active in this type of real estate are most likely to be best informed, along with real estate brokers, other businessmen and local officials in each particular area.

In recent years, state governments have stepped up their activities in land use planning and development controls; so, state commerce departments and other state agencies may well be a source of much useful data on ripe and soon-to-be-ripe areas.

Much can usually be learned about vacation-land development and potential by asking questions of people who already have invested profitably in that type of property, especially those who reside or operate a business in the area where they have invested, or who have invested heavily in a particular area. The names of such people can ordinarily be obtained from real estate agents in the areas concerned, from plat maps or tax rolls at local tax assessing offices or other local government offices, or from local businessmen. Another way to prospect for good buys is to find an ideally located piece of land, learn the owner's name from the tax polls, plat maps, section maps or other maps, and ask him if he'd like to sell. Detailed maps showing the names of owners are published by private firms in some areas; real estate agencies can give you the names of such firms, and may even be able to supply such maps themselves.

Evaluating the development potential of a vacation-land fringe area is less complex than for a suburban area; fewer kinds of development are involved. Demand for industrial, office or multiple dwelling uses is relatively limited, except for a trend toward condominium apartments in seashore areas. Most vacation-land development is for vacation homes, recreation, and the few kinds of businesses that serve tourists and vacationers—restaurants, bars, motels, gas stations, small grocery shops and general stores, boat liveries, sports equipment shops, amusement gimmicks, gift shops, and family recreation attractions like a miniature golf course.

What to Look For

The main thing to determine is how far in the future development is likely to be expanding fast enough to boost prices rapidly, and what the current status of development and development plans indicate about the answer to that question.

Once you have a line on a potentially fruitful area and are ready to take timely action to buy, you should focus on land whose particular location and characteristics make it most likely to rise in value swiftly within two to five years. Again, it's not just the fringe you want, but the choice spots on the fringe.

Any land that's destined to be developed for vacation or recreation use in the not-too-distant future is a good investment, but these are the types of vacation land that offer the best prospects for big profits quickly:

1. Lake Frontage, Seashore and River Frontage

Land bordering on water that's good for swimming, boating, fishing and other water sports is the most valuable of all vacation and recreation land. One reason for this is that it's scarce, which means this type of investment at a low price is not often easy to find. Lake lots in a development project may even appreciate in price after you buy them since the demand keeps growing faster than the supply, but the price is already so high that only a relatively small profit is likely.

Any water frontage where development is already well along commands a premium price, as does property on which a waterfront cottage or vacation home already stands. You can do fairly well if you buy early in the development stages, but you can never do as well as you can in lake frontage that's barely on the verge of development and is still low-priced.

Such land can still be found in places like Michigan's Upper Peninsula, where vacation land development only recently began to gain real momentum. When I paid $33.33 a foot on Pike Lake, it was already impossible to find any lake frontage for less than $100 a foot in the Lower Peninsula.

Any length of frontage is usually worth buying, except that less than 40 or 50 feet may not have much resale value, and may not be suitable for building purposes under local zoning codes. Also, it's best to buy as much as you can for the money you have to work with in order to get the most leverage.

2. Low-Priced Acreage in Medium-Sized Parcels on a Road

Vacation fringe land priced from $25 to $50 an acre offers the best crack at big profits in a short time. Land in this price range affords the best balance between the advantages of low-price leverage and relative certainty of sharp value rises in the near future.

At $25 an acre, such land is usually on the brink of having its price driven up by the approach of development. How soon or how fast, however, is still quite variable and is not easy to predict. Land's climbing above $25 and approaching $50, on the other hand, is a sign that prices are entering a fast-rise phase while you still have powerful low-price leverage. You can also make good profits on land up to $200 and even $300 an acre, but not as easily or quickly.

This fringe buying tactic works most effectively in parcels of about 40 acres to about 200 acres, or, if the price is low enough, up to 400 acres. Other things being equal, prices are higher for smaller parcels and you have less flexibility. Larger parcels are harder to buy, also entail less flexibility, and are harder to sell. Medium-sized tracts are usually attractive to all types of buyers, including developers, other predevelopment investors, and even ultimate users like a hunting club or lodge. You can also split them up into smaller parcels, yourself, with little difficulty.

In any case, parcels located on a road are preferable by far, since they are more likely to come into demand soon than land to which access is less convenient. Land not on a road is usually farther away from development, and predicting when development will reach it is riskier. Though such land is usually lower in price, comparable land on a road is better. And the better the road, the better the chances for an early price climb.

3. Land with Good Prospects for Commercial Use

Relatively less land is developed for commercial or business purposes in a vacation or resort area than in a growing suburb, since the population density is smaller and the seasonal nature of business makes the return on entrepreneurial investment more variable. There's also relatively little need for industrial or office property.

But there is still a need for small stores, restaurants, motels, bars and other tourist and vacation businesses. These most often require land fronting on main highways, especially on the fringe of a growing resort town, on or near a lake, seashore or other recreational water, or near an Interstate highway interchange.

Smaller parcels, from an acre to three or four—occasionally even less, as for some fast-food outlets—are most in demand. But a large tract of 40 to 100 acres that includes road frontage with commercial prospects is an especially lucky find.

4. Large Tracts of Low-Priced Acreage

Tracts of 300 acres and more, up to several square miles, can be bought in many parts of the country at inexpensive prices. These can be good investments if you have the money to handle them and the land lends itself to easy parceling, or you have solid reason to believe a developer will shortly be after it.

But large parcels present special problems that are grounds for caution. You have a lot of money tied up in, and riding on, one investment. Secondly, the range of potential buyers is limited by the total price, even if the price per acre is small. Thirdly, such tracts can be difficult to sell off in portions without costly subdivision procedures or development expenses unless all parts of the tract are close to an existing road, which is rare.

5. Smaller Parcels, Lots and Improved Property

Prices generally are higher, buyers are limited for the most part to ultimate users, and profits are smaller, but you can still derive some gain from 20-acre parcels, 10-acre pieces, 5-acre plots and smaller bits of ground, including lots and improved property containing a cottage or other structure. That is, if you buy carefully during the early stages of development while there's still potential for enough increase in demand to make further price rises likely.

Parcels of 10 or 20 acres are not big enough for profitable splitting into smaller parcels unless there is considerable road frontage, which few such parcels have. Prospects for resale to a developer are not good, either, unless you know about one that's packaging small parcels for a big development. Most developers prefer to buy large tracts at lower prices.

Such parcels, especially the 5-acre size, are in the end not much better than a small lot—from an investment standpoint. Your potential sales are pretty much restricted to ultimate users rather than developers or other predevelopment investors.

Nevertheless, you can make some profits in this type of land. I know some people who bought 2½-acre lots in a modest vacation-land project a few years ago and enjoyed a doubling in the value of their lots, thanks to the feverish growth of demand. They paid about $1,000 a lot and today 1½-acre lots in that development are selling for almost $3,000.

Why the Boom Will Last for Many a Year

The exploding demand for vacation recreation land is still in its early stages. Though some say it's too hot not to cool down, any cooling will be only temporary. The impact of America's suddenly discovered and frantically growing desire for such land has only begun to be felt. What's taken place so far will look like a baby's first wobbly step compared to the galloping growth yet to come over the next 50 to 100 years, bringing with it a windfall of big-profit opportunities as each fringe is overtaken by development and new fringes appear in ever-increasing numbers.

One of the prime forces behind the mushrooming demand for country and resort land is a growing American compulsion to escape the crime, smog, congestion and other ills of the city. People yearn for at least a respite, a brief fling in fresh air and pure water on weekends and vacations. Just as in their flight to suburbia, they'd rather own than rent—and they have the money to do it. Even camping enthusiasts want to get away from crowded campgrounds and park their campers on land of their own.

Developers of big land projects exploit this desire with advertising that offers an "escape hatch" or, as one slogan put it, "priceless protection from 'Big City' conditions." One ad for a Florida development said, "Trade city problems for a place in the Florida sun in peaceful Port Charlotte. Leave tension and trouble behind. Maybe you've dreamed about getting away from it all. The urban sprawl. Overcrowding. Noise. Pollution. Turmoil. Well, your getaway can be easier than you think."

Another project has billed itself as a "new and exciting rec-reational/residential community" that offers a "second home away from it all, where you can breathe clean air and unwind in the freshness of nature unspoiled. Where you have the freedom to spend leisure moments sanely and safely."

The repetition of this theme by land project promoters reinforces and adds momentum to Americans' growing desire for vacation homes of their own. Promising "escape from the city" has helped make the idea stylish and boost demand for vacation land of all kinds.

The New American Dream of a Second Home in the Country

Another powerful pressure behind the vacation-land boom arises from American affluence. Owning a second home in the country, a cabin in the mountains or a cottage on a lake, seems as normal today as owning one home seemed 25 years ago. In a 1971 survey of 1,000 newlywed couples in 42 states, 62 percent already were planning to buy a vacation retreat. "The land rush is powered in no small part by affluent people seeking second homes," said *Time* magazine in its Oct. 1, 1973, issue. "Rising affluence steadily demands more land per person. . . . Apartment dwellers no longer are content with a rented room by the seashore on their holidays; more and more yearn for their own cabin on Mosquito Lake."

Affluence, Recreation, and the Leisure Time Revolution

American affluence also is responsible for still another impetus behind the land boom; namely, the burgeoning interest in sports and recreation made possible by high personal incomes and increased leisure time. "More and more people are earning more and more money in their workaday worlds," said a land project ad in the *Wall Street Journal,* "and are simultaneously being given more and more spare time in which to escape from them." While interest grows phenomenally in camping, skiing, boating, fishing, swimming and snowmobiling, more and more Americans also are deciding they want to enjoy these activities on land of their own—or at least to own land near a lake or a ski slope. This trend also is exploited by the development firms, who dress up their projects with such enticements as ski slopes, golf courses, lakes, sandy beaches, tennis courts, clubhouses, fishing ponds and streams, horseback riding stables, park areas, snowmobile trails, and even yacht marinas.

A Growing Need for Retirement Comfort and Independence

Yet another force behind the booming demand for land is the need of a growing senior citizen population for places to live out their retirement years in comfort. Greater longevity, earlier retirement ages, and pension programs that provide the elderly with the resources to be independent all add fuel to the pressure for more living space. Many development projects, especially in the warm climate states, appeal especially to older buyers by picturing themselves as cozy places to retire. Many label themselves a "total community" that offers everything—escape from the city, a bonanza of recreation facilities, and retirement serenity besides.

The existence of booming land development projects in hundreds of areas across the United States is visible proof that the voracious, fast-growing appetite for vacation land is really just getting started. As America's population and economy continue to expand in the years to come, so will the need and demand for vacation and recreation land. As a development company executive said recently, "Recreation land is a tremendous growth area."

Economic downturns, energy crises and gasoline shortages may dampen the boom occasionally, but never for long. In some places, overexcited promotion may cause a bubble to burst, leaving price plunges in its wake. But for the most part and for many years into the future, continued increases in affluence, inflation, leisure time, the urge for urban escape, early retirement, and craving for recreation land will keep intensifying the demand for vacation land.

6

WHAT TO LOOK FOR
WHEN YOU'RE BUYING

Location is so important that it can make you money all by itself. An ordinary piece of land purchased at the going market price can produce a big profit in a short time just by being in the right spot—in the path of suddenly booming development or ideally situated for prime commercial use. You don't even have to work at selling it. Buyers come to you.

Bad location, on the other hand, can ruin your chances for easy sale or big profit—even in a growing area where most fringe investments are profitable. The cardinal rule in looking for a right location is to be sure to look. People who get stuck with a piece of swampland or desert several miles from the nearest road get into such a mess by failing to make a personal visit to the land before signing a contract or forking over a deposit. If there's any one thing that real estate experts agree on, it's that you should *never, never, never,* a thousand times *never,* buy land before you lay eyes on it.

There's no way you can make an intelligent judgment on a property's location, condition, flaws, potential use, surrounding development, price, and other characteristics and possible problems without inspecting it carefully, walking on it, examining its environs, checking what else in the vicinity is for sale, and getting every bit of pertinent information about it and its surrounding area that it is humanly possible to get.

Don't be like millions of Americans who buy land over the telephone, through the mail or from a fast-talking salesman at a "free dinner" promotion without first looking at what they're buying. Don't even make a "refundable" deposit. Land hustlers use a lot of tricks and high pressure tactics to lure you into a commitment of some kind before you see the land they're selling. Don't fall for any of them, no matter how innocent or fair they may seem on the surface.

What Can Happen if You Buy Blind

In a pamphlet entitled "Consumer Protection, Interstate Land Sales," the U.S. Department of Housing and Urban Development says:

> Too often, vacation and retirement sites are sold to eager out-of-state buyers who have not inspected the property.
>
> The warm sun in Florida and Arizona, and the cool woods in North Carolina and New England—far from the work-a-day world—help speed interstate land sales without on-the-spot inspection. The fact that lots may be paid for in small monthly installments tends to make buyers casual about checking on the properties.
>
> In a significant number of cases, buyers did not receive what they thought they were buying. Many purchases were based upon inadequate or misleading information. A development might be described as "10 miles from Rainbow City," without any indication that the 10 miles leads through an impassable swamp, and that it is 34 miles via passable roads. A lot may be described as "readily accessible" when it can be reached only by footpath or a car with four-wheel drive.

A New York surgeon once bought 5½ acres in Florida and when he finally went south to see the land ten years later, he discovered there was no easy way to get to it and the area was infested with poisonous snakes.

Of course, it's not a good idea to look for an investment in a development project in the first place. But such projects are not the only places where you might encounter pressures to buy blindly. Other sellers use such tactics, too. The rule to keep always in mind is never to buy without first looking at the land; never buy under pressure, either. In fact, you shouldn't even buy after only one look. Never be impatient. It's important to take the time to inspect the land thoroughly and learn every important fact that bears on its profitability—*before* you buy.

If anyone is trying hard to sell something to you, it's probably not a good buy—unless he's trying so hard that he reduces the price considerably. When a piece of land is a good buy, the seller doesn't have to push hard to sell it. If he doesn't know it's a good buy, it should not be difficult to bring the price down. Good investments don't come looking for you. You have to go looking for them.

Shopping for Good Buys

After you've lined up an area or a few properties that seem worth investigating, make arrangements to see them. If the land is some distance away, you might schedule visits to several parcels on one trip—possibly include them on a family vacation jaunt.

The first source of details is the owner, or the real estate agent. Learn everything possible from him about the property, its potential, other available property in the area, the area's development history and trends, and other points important to price appreciation prospects. Never hesitate to request information or ask a question for fear of sounding dumb. It's better to sound dumb than to be dumb. It costs less than buying the wrong land.

When you're looking at land advertised in a newspaper or brought to your attention by a real estate agent, keep your eyes peeled also for other "For Sale" signs. Once you get the feel of land investment shopping, your eye becomes alert to opportunities and you can learn much about an area and available properties just by driving around. You'll be surprised at the things you never noticed before.

In the beginning, it's a good idea to shop for a while, and in more than one area, before you make your first investment. You will be able to move more promptly and with confidence after you acquire a "feel" for spotting good buys quickly. You should always be patient and careful, and never move hastily for fear you might miss a good buy. You won't run out of opportunities. If you miss one, there are plenty more. It's less costly to miss a good opportunity out of caution than to hurry into a mistake. On the other hand, of course, it gains you nothing to be so overcautious that you never buy. Once you get started, you will gradually develop a sense of balance on this—of how careful to be, when to make a move, and when to break the rules. Until you've gained some experience, however, it's better to be a bit too cautious than not cautious enough.

Real estate agents can be quite helpful during this scouting phase of the operation. Sometimes you can get a lower price by purchasing directly from an owner rather than through an agent, since the owner has no commission to pay. It's usually easier to buy without going through an agent, too, than selling without the help of one. But an agent can offer valuable help in finding a good investment. He knows about most land for sale in an area, even if not all —especially if he's a member of a cooperative multi-listing service with other brokers in the area, which is quite common. However, make sure it's you who makes the decision on what to buy, not he, and that you decide according to facts. Also, you need not feel obligated to buy through an agent just because he's been helpful. The key thing is what you buy.

Three Crucial Points about Location

There are three characteristics of primary importance to keep in mind when shopping for a good investment on the fringes of suburban and vacation land growth. These are:

1. Roads

Commerce, manufacturing and other development have always sprouted and thrived where transportation is convenient, whether by ship, railroad, wagon train, or automobile. Today, the most important ingredient in location is convenient access to a highway, especially with regard to commercial use.

Land almost always rises faster and higher in price when it's on a road, and that's practically a prerequisite for commercial use. Such land is more likely to be developed soon than land that can be reached only over a difficult path or is "landlocked" (access is not possible except across someone else's land).

Land on a paved road is usually a better investment than land on a gravel road, if price is about the same. Land on a corner of two paved roads is more valuable yet, and so is land next to a freeway interchange. For land on a side street or secondary road, nearness to a main road is a factor. Land on a road that doesn't look like much, but promises to blossom into importance soon, is what you're looking for. Land away from any road is cheaper, but probably will take longer to rise in value and not rise as high.

Location on a main road is not so desirable for residential purposes, but that is not a high-value use. Location on a good road, even if not a main one, is important in medium-sized tracts of vacation land. When finally developed for use, vacation land is most valuable off a main road, but not far from one. The ideal is to be remote enough to feel fresh, rustic and relaxingly away from crowds, but not so remote as to be hard to reach.

2. Water

Land on an ocean, lake or river has always been more coveted, more valuable than most other land—for farming, commerce, transportation, and now, more than ever, swimming, boating, fishing and lazing on the beach.

Real estate next to water that's suitable for recreation purposes always commands a premium price. If there's anything more scarce than land, it's lakes. The next most valuable recreation and vacation land is that which is near water, or within convenient reach.

3. Distance

A suburban property's potential value depends not only on its distance from current development, but its specific distance from such things as shopping centers, freeways, schools, parks, factories and residential developments. Distance, in this case, means not only the number of miles, but also convenience of access. If a property is near a shopping center, but there's a railroad track in between, and the nearest crossing is two miles out of the way, the effective distance is far greater than the actual measurement as the crow flies. Also important is the distance from anticipated new construction of stores, etc.

In vacation land, distance from the nearest community, stores, recreation areas and expected new development is important. To have good prospects for appreciation in the near future, land should be within one day's drive of a major population center, or several smaller centers.

Conditions and Characteristics for Careful Checking

Some special circumstances—like nearness to water, a shopping center under construction, or a new Disney World— can mean sharp value increases. Others, however, can detract from value, and they are just as vital. It's important to know about them before you buy, not after. If there's anything about a piece of land that tends to lower its value but which is not immediately obvious, it's not likely that the seller will volunteer the information. You have to get it, yourself.

After preliminary shopping produces a promising piece or two of land, it's time for a serious investigation. In addition to meticulous physical examination of the land and its vicinity, there are records to check and people to talk to about the land and the area, including owners of nearby property, residents, businessmen, real estate agents, builders, bankers, utility officials, developers, attorneys, and local authorities who handle taxes, property records, public health, water supply, sewer service, roads, land use planning and zoning.

It doesn't take as much work and time as it may seem. Once you get started and get the hang of it, it gets easy quickly. It doesn't take long to build a foundation of knowledge about an area that enables you to know at once what details you need, how to get them efficiently, what to look for, and how to evaluate a property with speed and accuracy.

The specifics you should consider when evaluating a particular piece of land can be listed under three general categories for checklist purposes, as follows:

1. Physical Condition and Characteristics

A. *Size and Shape*. Be sure not to buy an awkward size or shape that might interfere with profitable use, especially with regard to the use you have in mind. Commercial spots can range from half an acre for a small store to 150 acres for a giant shopping center. Parcels from three to eight acres may be suitable for a small shopping center or discount store, but only if there is enough road frontage. A six-acre parcel in an area where only 20 percent of it on a road is suitable for commercial use may leave you with a big portion that can't be used profitably. On the other hand, the rest of it might be feasible for apartments. The important thing is to check out the potential uses for the size and location. As to shape, straight boundaries and square corners are preferable. Stay away from irregular shapes; they may be difficult to make full or effective use of. I know of some vacation land developments offering 10-acre lots that are almost half a mile long and only 200 feet wide. Ridiculous. My 80 acres in Kalkaska was half a mile deep from the road, but had a quarter of a mile frontage, which is all right. When buying on a road, as is usually wise, make sure the depth is neither so great as to give you a lot of useless land, nor so shallow that use is unduly restricted.

B. *Terrain.* Is it flat, rolling, sloped or marred by sharp drops? Flat land is almost always easier to use without costly alterations, and therefore it is more valuable. However, that's not inevitably the case with vacation land. Whether building can take place immediately and whether the terrain would hamper the potential use you're counting on are two important questions to be answered.

C. *Trees, underbrush, etc.* Is the land usable as is, or will it need a lot of clearing first? Is the beach sandy or covered with rocks? In vacation land, of course, good foliage is usually desirable.

D. *Soil.* Can it support the intended use? Will local health officials permit installation of septic tanks if no sewer system exists? Ask them. Have "perc tests" been conducted in the area to determine how much sewage the ground can safely absorb, and how many structures with septic tanks can be built per acre?

E. *Water.* If it's the wrong kind, like swampy conditions or poor storm drainage, it can detract from land values. Value also can suffer if there's no public water supply system and wells bring up poor water, or the ground water is insufficient. Check for low, water-collecting spots that might be troublesome or require landfill operations before the land can be used. Is the land lower than adjacent land so that it would get its rainwater runoff? If the land is on a lake, is its water clean? Is it filled with tree trunks and debris? Is there a stream on the land? If it's on a river, is the bank marshy or firm? In a suburban area, check for availability of water from a public supply system. If none is there, no development is likely to take place until there is. In a vacation area, it's the well water situation that's important. What's it like and how deep are the wells? Check with local water department and health department officials. In a suburban area, if no supply mains serve the land, ask when construction is anticipated.

F. *Sewers.* Access to public sanitary sewers also is important to suburban development. Find out from local officials whether sewer lines extend to the land and, if not, how far away from it they are and how soon they'll get there. Are there any use restrictions in effect because of no sewers? This may be important for such use as apartments. Septic tanks may be permitted in many areas for single-family dwellings, but practically never for apartments—and never for any residential development. However, development of large tracts for houses does not depend on pre-existence of sewer lines, as the installation of sewers usually is part of the development process. Nevertheless, land contemplated for such development must be near a sewer system to which its new lines can be connected.

G. *Utilities.* Is electric power service available? Natural Gas? Telephone lines? In suburbia, these are essential and usually are available, except that in some areas natural gas lines are not yet installed or no new tap-ins are permitted. The opposite is often true on the vacation land fringe. Electric service is the most important, and if lines haven't reached the land yet, find out from the local power company how far away they are and how soon they're likely to be extended to the land you're interested in. I neglected to check that out with regard to my Pike Lake frontage, where there's still no electricity. Fortunately, it hasn't seemed to matter much; and when the electricity does arrive, that will boost land values further. As a rule, it's not good to buy land that doesn't have electric service unless you learn that it's definitely scheduled to get there soon.

H. *Access.* If it's not on a good road, can you get to the land easily? In winter as well as summer? Ask the people who live there. Concerning suburban land, are there any peculiar access problems caused by unusual conditions like a railroad track or limited access freeway?

I. *Boundaries.* Are they clearly marked so you can find them easily? Make sure there are no confusions or disagreements over boundaries among neighbors or in legal documents. If you see any potential trouble spots, ask the seller to provide a survey.

J. *Erosion.* This can happen along an ocean or lake shore. Ask real estate agents in the area about it and check with local officials, especially those dealing with environmental matters.

K. *Current use.* Is the land being used for anything now that might adversely affect future use and potential profit? Ask real estate agents, builders and developers.

L. *Special characteristics.* Does it have a hill that would make a great ski slope? Or a big ditch in front that would have to be filled?

2. Characteristics of the Vicinity and Surrounding Area

A. *Road conditions.* If the land is on a road, is it the kind of road that's suitable for the intended use? Is the road maintained well? What are the plans of local officials for improving or upgrading the road, and other roads nearby, and how are they likely to affect the potential use and value of the land? Land on a secondary road that has high probability of being converted soon by widening or other improvements into a main thoroughfare, can be a superb investment. If the land is not on a road, how far from a road is it and how soon is there likely to be a road built that does reach it? How far is the land, on a road or not, from a major artery like a freeway or other main highway?

B. *Distance from water, recreation and other facilities.* If the land is not on a lake, river or seashore, how far away from recreational water is it? As far as vacation land is concerned, how far is it from a big city, from a permanent community of any size, from stores, from a ski resort, from hunting areas, from tourist attractions, from other recreation facilities? In suburban land, the important distances are those from shopping centers, from schools and other signs of population density, and from such things as airports or trash dumps that might in some cases detract from value.

C. *Condition and usage of adjoining and nearby land.* Is the vicinity conducive to the kind of development and use you need in order for your land to appreciate in value significantly? For instance, a gravel pit close by might well hamper prospects for many kinds of commercial use. Is nearby land swampy or in otherwise poor condition? That can affect the attractiveness of the land you're considering even if it's in fine shape, itself. The surrounding poorer land may also dominate and restrict the entire area's character and use. If you can't tell just by looking, be sure to ask real estate agents, businessmen and property owners in the area if there are any unseen problems that might interfere with the desirability of the land.

D. *Development.* How far away is it? What kind is it? Which direction has it been taking in the past few years? Which direction is it expected to take from now on, or being forced to take by local planners and zoning boards? How fast has development been moving and are there any reasons to expect a change? What kinds of construction are underway? On the drawing boards? Being promoted by developers and wheeler-dealers? What plans for expansion do local retailers and other businesses have? What is the current status of the local construction industry? Have new housing starts fallen off or stepped up? What about new apartments, office buildings, gas stations, restaurants and stores? In suburban areas, find out where the next shopping centers are likely to be built, where developers are getting ready to break ground for new residential subdivisions, and where other new structures are about to be built or have begun to appear. In vacation land areas, look for signs of growth in the nearest towns, such as new restaurants, new motels, and new gas stations, as well as for new cottages near the lake or in the mountains and such evidence of development as big billboards advertising lake lots. If you can't make a clear-cut determination by looking, talk to real estate agents, builders, developers, other businessmen and local government officials.

E. *Economic conditions.* Is the area's economy booming or depressed? On what industry is it most dependent and what is the outlook for it? Is the area losing industry and jobs, or gaining? Are there signs that growth may be about to stop rather than continue? What kind of effort does the community put into attracting and keeping business and industry? In vacation land areas, does the local community try to encourage growth? Is the area going downhill or does it look like fertile ground for a boom?

F. *Property sales.* How's the real estate business doing in the area? Are people buying? How have prices been acting? If buyer interest seems to have increased recently, that may well be a sign of a good time to buy.

G. *Special situations.* The announcement and later the construction of a giant new amusement park or a New Town in the countryside is almost like setting up an additional metropolitan center from which growth radiates outward. This means a whole new set of opportunities. Other extraordinary developments or characteristics in an area can also affect land values enormously, such as the discovery of large oil deposits in northern Michigan a few years ago, or plans for creation of a national park. Be alert to such possibilities.

3. Regulations, Restrictions and Other Possible Problems

A. *Zoning*. Most communities have a zoning system and a map showing the kinds of uses permitted on their land. Be sure to get a copy of the map so you can determine the potential for rezoning to higher use as well as the current situation. How does the zoning restrict current use? Does the current zoning appear to be final, like commercial or industrial? Or transitional, like agricultural? If it's residential, you may need to check further to determine if that's intended to be the final use or is considered to be only tentative depending on the course and nature of development. How difficult is it to get a zoning change? Find out what recent practice has been. Does the local government have a master plan for land use, and how often does it make changes in it, and why? Who are the people in the area who influence development and can give you a realistic idea of how much change is possible or likely? Find out by asking real estate agents, planning officials, developers and builders.

B. *Development controls*. Suburban communities frequently impose minimum lot size restrictions and other regulations on development in addition to zoning. State governments are becoming more active in controlling vacation land development, especially where local governments take the attitude that any growth is good. Such controls may prohibit development altogether in some areas, impose strict platting requirements, or restrict construction because of soil or drainage conditions. Be sure you check with local authorities on such matters to determine the effect they have on any land you might buy.

C. *Use restrictions*. There may also be additional prohibitions and limitations in local building codes, zoning rules, health department regulations and other ordinances. Restrictions on building height or size, for instance, might prevent a potential commercial use that would be otherwise suitable and profitable. Rules on the number of lots or buildings per acre, on setbacks from the road, on distance between buildings and property lines, and on driveways or other access to the road, may be crucial. Sometimes use restrictions, in the zoning code or elsewhere, can be valuable. If you figure a parcel to be potentially suitable for an expensive restaurant, a prohibition on mobile home courts and junkyards may be welcome. Perceiving ahead of others where land between a commercial zone and a one-family residential area will have limited use can lead you to a good investment, since such land can be developed as a "buffer zone" of apartments. It's important also to be alert to the chances that future freeway construction or other new structures or uses nearby will impose new use restrictions on the land you're considering. In any case, it's wise to learn as much about all relevant zoning, use and construction regulations—and probable or potential changes in them—before you buy, rather than be surprised by them later. (Another place to check for possible use restrictions is the subdivision plat, if the land has already been subdivided. Also, there occasionally are use restrictions in a property's deed, which can be ascertained in a title search or examination of the abstract, a necessary step before completing a sale.)

D. *Clear title and other legal aspects*. The most expeditious approach to learning the important facts about a property's legal history and any flaws or potential flaws in its title, such as liens against it, is to obtain a commitment of title insurance from a title insurance company. In most transactions, it is agreed that it should be the seller's responsibility to provide such evidence of clear title at his expense. If the seller balks at doing so, be wary. There may be something he doesn't want you to know. If his only objection to a title insurance commitment or title search, however, is the cost, it's not uncommon for that to be subject to negotiation. In some places, it's traditional for the buyer to bear at least some of the cost for verifying clear title.

Among the things you want to know are whether the seller owns the land free and clear, whether he's buying it on a land contract and does not yet have title, whether there are others who share ownership or have another legal interest in the land such as a lease or an easement, and whether there are any tax liens or other claims against the land. Much of this you or your attorney can learn from local property and tax records, but it's much easier to do it through a title insurance firm that knows how to go through the procedures efficiently and already has a backlog of documents and information on file. It's often worth doing that even if you have to pay for it. The practice of obtaining title insurance has replaced the old method of having an attorney laboriously examine an abstract of title showing a property's legal history. Another advantage is that if the title insurance firm makes a mistake, it's the loser, not you. If your attorney makes a mistake in his examination of a title abstract, on the other hand, that's the same as if you make it. In some remote areas on the vacation-land fringe, however, title insurance has not yet replaced examination of abstracts.

Among the specifics to watch are whether a utility company has an easement that would enable it to build a power line or a gas pipeline across the land, and whether the mineral rights go with the title or are reserved to someone else who can dig up the land or drill for oil whenever he wants.

Never buy land without a title insurance commitment or other assurance of clear title. When making a deposit or signing an offer or sales agreement before that base is covered, be sure to make the agreement contingent on satisfactory evidence of clear title. When signing a land contract providing that you get title only after completing the payments, be sure to get the title protection at the beginning when you sign the contract committing yourself to the purchase; don't wait until you've completed the payments and are about to get a deed, for it may be too late then. If you wish to check a property's title and tax situation even before making a deposit, you can inspect recorded deeds, land contracts, tax liens and other documents at the county register of deeds or recorder's office. These are public records and usually someone there will be glad to show you how to get the information you want from their files. Filing systems vary widely and many places now have such records on microfilm. Remember, however, that you cannot make as thorough a check as an attorney or title expert.

When You Should Have an Attorney

It is possible to buy and sell land without the services of a real estate broker or an attorney and not suffer any ill consequences. But I don't recommend it. You can, for instance, contact a title insurance firm without an attorney's help or anyone else's. But a real estate broker can usually take care of such details more efficiently than you can, yourself, and an attorney performs important services that you shouldn't try to do yourself. It's often wise to have an attorney review all documents and agreements, including the title insurance, even when a real estate broker is involved. This is especially true when you are inexperienced in land investments, and when the only real estate broker involved is representing the other party to the transaction. (Sometimes two brokers are involved, one representing the seller and one the buyer.)

It's also especially important to have an attorney make sure that you're getting what you think you're getting when a transaction is complicated or large amounts of money are involved. You need to know exactly what your rights and obligations are in any contract, exactly what effect any flaws or restrictions in a property's legal status may have on your ownership or profit potential, and exactly what everything else in the documents mean. A real estate agent can be quite helpful, but an attorney is most knowledgeable. An attorney can be necessary on occasion when you're selling land, too; but he's especially vital when you're buying.

As you gain experience and knowledge in land investments, you will get a clearer idea of what you can handle without an attorney. But you also will discover how helpful and necessary one is. Instances arise where you want your attorney to prepare contracts and agreements to suit you, rather than just review those drawn up by others.

Better Too Many Facts Than Too Few

All this may seem like a staggering amount of information to get, a mind-boggling number of points to cover, and a fearsome array of possible pitfalls to avoid. But it's not really difficult or as time-consuming to handle as it may appear. Once you get started, you will quickly acquire a foundation of basic knowledge about an area, or several areas, that you will not have to relearn every time you consider a particular piece of land. You will also learn shortcuts, such as how to get information on several aspects in one place. Though there's no central depository of real estate investment information or of data on a particular area's real estate, you will find through experience where the most informative sources are (usually certain real estate firms and certain local officials or agencies).

As you go along, you also will gain a "feel" for how much information you need in each case to make a good evaluation and shrewd decision. Ordinarily, it's better to have too much information than too little, but you don't want to waste a lot of time gathering extraneous details, either. Making proper use of the information is the main thing. No piece of land is perfect, so it's vital to calculate accurately the probable impact of the imperfections; then, if you figure the land is still a good buy, make use of them to negotiate a lower price.

7

HOW TO GET A
BETTER THAN RIGHT PRICE

If there's anything as important as location and potential use, it's price. Paying too much can be a worse mistake than bad location.

If you pay more for land than it's worth, it could take a long time for its value to catch up with your error. You may not lose in the end, but you'll have to wait longer for less profit and there's more time for something to go wrong.

Instant Profit from a Low Enough Price

On the other hand, you can profit immediately by getting a price lower than the current market value. When you buy below the market price range, you can turn around and sell at a profit at once, without waiting for value to appreciate. This works with just about any real estate, of course, not just raw land. You can always make money by buying cheap and selling dear.

Take, for example, the lake frontage I bought in Michigan's Upper Peninsula. The asking price was $50 per front foot and I paid $33.33. If $50 was the going market value, I could have put the land up for sale again right away and made a 50 percent profit quickly. If the market value had been only $40, I could still have made about 20 percent. These figures are based on having paid for the land in full with cash. Since I bought on a land contract with a partial down payment, leverage would have increased the profit percentages markedly.

A relative of mine recently came upon a piece of vacation land worth $6,000 on the market and was able to buy it for only $4,000 with some shrewd bargaining. He planned to put it up for sale again at $6,500.

Whether or not you plan to resell soon, you should always make a determined effort to buy below market value. This for all practical purposes eliminates any remaining shred of risk there might be in buying land, since raw land values hardly ever fall. Prices may drop if they exceed true value, but actual values rarely do.

Among the advantages of real estate as an investment is that its price is usually subject to negotiation, which makes it generally easier to acquire at prices below true market value. Your own skill and stamina as a bargainer can be decisive factors, and a seller's particular circumstances can be made to work in your favor whether or not you are aware of them.

No Time to Be Reasonable

You want to have realistic knowledge of the fair market value, though not because that's what you should pay. You want to know how high not to go. The object is to get the lowest possible price. Sometimes a piece of land is a superb investment at its market value or even its asking price because its location is so excellent and its prospects for rapid price rises so close to certain. But ordinarily you should hesitate to buy if you can't get a better than right price.

Getting the lowest possible price requires a commitment never to be timid or reasonable. If you don't like to haggle over price, if you think you should be reasonable or fair, or if it bothers you that you might hurt someone's feelings by offering an absurdly low price, then you probably should stay out of land investment.

Being reasonable almost never gets the lowest possible price. You don't need to be rude or unpleasant; that's not the idea. You can be polite and friendly while remaining, underneath, granite firm in businesslike refusal to pay more than an unreasonably low price. You must be genuinely willing to get up and walk out if you're not getting a good price, to let a fairly good deal escape if you can't turn it into a really good deal.

This is not to say you never yield, compromise, or raise your original offer. The technique is merely the traditional bargaining strategy of the buyer; namely, starting out low enough so that your offer is sure not to be accepted, then going up grudgingly while applying pressure on the seller to come down in price with such tactics as pointing out the property's flaws and arguing that it is he who is being unreasonable.

Never become anxious, or let it show if you do. Take the nonchalant attitude that there are plenty of other good land investments around at better prices, which may well be true. Here is another spot where a real estate agent can help you if he's representing you rather than the seller. Let him do the haggling while you call the signals from the sidelines.

It's true you may lose a few deals that way, as I failed to get the 200 acres in Michigan's Upper Peninsula by refusing to pay as much down as the seller wanted. But most deals aren't that good, anyway, if you can't get the right price.

Even if you do miss an opportunity or two that turns out to have been worth the high price (prices sometimes go up so fast that what seemed too high five years ago is five times higher today), it's still better to err in that direction than to pay too much. For one thing, there are indeed plenty of other opportunities, many of them better than the one you missed. Overall, operating this way always pays off because it averages out to lower prices and higher profits.

Profiting from Desperation and Lack of Knowledge

It's also a sure way to take advantage of any unknown desperation on the seller's part. Sometimes a seller is in a hurry to sell for a reason you don't know and might never suspect. It could be an urgent need for cash, a divorce settlement, or a business crisis that's pressuring him to accept a lower price than he would if he could take his time. He surprises you with a quick acceptance of a low offer, or capitulates early in the bargaining. But this can't happen if you don't give it a chance by making a low offer.

I know of a case in which a piece of prime suburban land was on the market for $25,000, but an investor bought it for only $10,000 because the seller was desperate for cash. When another buyer offered the investor $15,000, he laughed. A few years later he sold it to a bank for $150,000. He could have turned a big profit quickly if he had wanted, but decided to hold onto it a while, since it cost him so little. His ability to get a low price made him an extra $15,000 when he did sell.

In the case in which my relative bought $6,000 worth of vacation land for $4,000, he sensed from the seller's offer to take only $5,000 in a cash deal that he urgently needed the cash. So he offered only $4,000 cash, and it was accepted.

Another investor bought a $17,500 property for $10,000 cash because the owners were getting a divorce and wanted a quick cash sale so they could make their settlement. Two weeks later the buyer sold it for $14,000.

These deals were possible because the buyer could offer cash. Though lower prices can also be negotiated in installment purchases, better buys are usually available more often when you can pay cash—which you can do even when you don't have the cash, if you can borrow it, with or without the property you're buying as collateral.

Sometimes you may have information about a seller's anxiety and can take advantage of it. Or there may be ways to find out. But that's not necessary. All you need to do is take the simple step of offering a very low price and see what happens. If you can't bring yourself to do that, you won't do as well in land investment. You might still make good profits, but they won't be as big and the danger of making mistakes is greater.

The next best thing to seller desperation, from a buyer's point of view, is seller ignorance. It's easier to get a low price from a seller who doesn't know the prevailing prices and market values. One reason why it's not an advantage to buy through a real estate agent is that he is likely to be knowledgeable about prices. He also is likely to know more than a seller about growth patterns, bargaining tactics and other aspects. This applies primarily to cases where the owner is selling through a real estate agent. If an agent is helping you look for an investment and represents you in a purchase, he should protect your interests, including low price, even though a higher price means a bigger commission for him.

The Slippery Thing Called Market Value

In order to know what price to stay under, you need a realistic understanding of true market value—or, to be more precise, the market value range. Market value is the point at which a willing buyer and a willing seller can reach agreement. What makes this tricky is that the point can vary widely with different sellers and buyers. Some sellers are willing to accept less than others. Some buyers are willing to pay more.

One way to pin it down more firmly is to say market value is the price on which a reasonable buyer and a reasonable seller can agree. But how can you tell what a reasonable buyer would pay before he pays it? Or what a reasonable seller would accept before he accepts it? No one can know for sure. You can only estimate.

Estimating market value is such an important part of real estate that it is a separate branch; namely, the profession of property appraising. Also known as realty valuation, appraising is based on certain principles and procedures that supposedly make it a reliable system based on facts and logic.

The flaw in this is that reasonable men can disagree. When ten professional appraisers go out to estimate the market value of a property, and all ten are eminently reasonable and qualified, it's still probable that they will come back with ten different appraisals. One way to overcome this lack of precision, however, is to figure an average of the estimates. Another way is to view them as a "range" in which most reasonable buyers and sellers would probably find agreement.

Basic Methods of Appraisal

There are several different appraisal methods and some disagreement within the profession over which are most reliable in different situations. The three most commonly used are:

1. Estimation of market value based on comparisons with the sale prices of similar property.

2. The physical or cost approach, based on what it would cost to replace the land and its structures.

3. The economic or income approach premised on net return from current use or anticipated return from potential use.

These sometimes overlap, and often more than one method is used to reach a balanced result in one appraisal.

The physical or cost approach is not pertinent to raw land. It is concerned mostly with the cost of reproducing such physical facilities as buildings—a matter primarily of the cost of labor and materials.

The economic or income approach can be pertinent, however, though rarely in terms of current income. It can be used to calculate the present value of potential future income.

In appraising raw land, the market value estimate—the least complex of appraisal methods—is the most commonly used. The major element is a matter of supply and demand; namely, what other land of a similar nature in the area is priced at, and what it has been selling for. The key word is "comparables"—the price and sales facts about nearby parcels that are comparable in location, potential use, and current value.

How to Get the Facts on Comparables

It's usually impossible to find another parcel that's exactly the same. The idea is to find land with as many similarities as possible and calculate adjustments for differences in location, condition, amount of road frontage, potential use, and other aspects.

The most reliable comparables are actual sales of similar land. The price that someone actually paid is more indicative of true market value than a price that an owner is asking but might not get. Unfortunately, actual sales are usually not as plentiful and information about them is not always easy to get.

Asking prices can be learned just by inquiring at realty offices and calling the phone numbers on "For Sale" signs. But, as for actual sales, there often haven't been many recently, and adjusting for time difference and intervening changes in the case of older sales is a matter of additional guesswork that makes older comparables less relevant. Also, buyers, sellers, and realty firms are reluctant to give information on recent sales to anyone except professional appraisers and others in the real estate field. They like to keep such facts confidential and exclusive.

The easiest way to surmount this obstacle is to retain an appraiser, preferably one who is familiar with the area and who has no other interest in the transaction. You should be able to count on him to be impartial and objective—though, of course, not too impartial and objective. You want him to remember that you as buyer would prefer a figure on the low end of the market value range. An appraisal can be inexpensive when only raw land is involved. If a great deal of money is involved in an intended purchase and it's difficult to get a clear idea of market value on your own, a professional appraisal is in order.

Researching Documents on Your Own

You can get information on comparables, yourself, if you want, and you probably ought to do so at least once just to understand how it's done. Start by visiting realty offices in the area to get as much data as you can. Don't just ask about recent sales, but express interest in buying and raise questions about recent sales while discussing prices. You may be able to extract useful information on a follow-up visit if a broker or his salesman is cagey the first time you show up asking questions. Many real estate agents, however, may be willing to discuss recent sales freely.

You can also learn much on your own at the county register of deeds office, recorder's office, or other local government office in charge of maintaining property records and tax records. Each such office usually has a different system of record keeping and employees there ordinarily will be glad to show you how to find the documents you want to see. They can show you how to cross-check between maps and records, and how to find the records for the properties you're checking. If you're not sure what documents are likely to contain the information you want, they can usually be helpful on that, too. Such records are all public records and you have a right to see them. The same is true of records in your local tax assessor's and treasurer's office.

Reading the Documents and the Tax Stamp Code

The price at which a piece of land was sold at its most recent changing of ownership can usually be found on the recorded deed or land contract. However, it's not always simple.

Parties to a real estate transaction sometimes wish to hinder discovery of the sale price by others. In such cases, the deed will describe the sale price as "$1 and other valuable consideration," or something similar that omits the specific price. In most states, you can still determine the sales price by the tax stamps affixed to the deed, but it will require some basic information and a bit of calculation.

Most states have a transfer tax on real estate conveyances that must be paid before a deed can be recorded. Payment of this tax is evidenced by stamps affixed to the deed, reflecting the amount of tax paid. Since the tax is usually a percentage of the sale price, the sale price can be calculated if you know the percentage. In Ohio, for instance, the tax is $1 per $1,000. So, if there are $20 worth of tax stamps on a deed, you multiply $1,000 times 20 to learn the price was $20,000. Michigan has a similar system, though the percentage may differ. You can check your state's system and percentage at the nearest property records office.

In the case of land contracts, the price and terms are always specified. A problem sometimes encountered with these, however, is that the buyer may not have the contract recorded, even though he should do so for his own protection.

Though an appraiser or a real estate agent has the experience and knowledge to do this kind of research more efficiently, he is not likely to do it for you unless you pay him or he's sure you'll buy from him. Doing it yourself is time-consuming at first, though after you learn how easy it is, you will be able to get the information you want quickly.

Before I bought land north of Detroit several years ago, I did some research in the county property records and found that the owner had paid $9,000 for it a few years earlier. I also checked comparables in the area and found that the price of $40 per front foot for 225 feet on the highway was lower than other prices. So, when the owner declined to accept less than $9,000 even though he needed cash for his laundry business, I made the deal because I knew it was a good price.

Later, when the state highway department condemned most of the site and I went to court to get more than the $9,000 I was offered, I made a thorough and meticulous research into comparable values and that helped me get $11,000 from the condemnation jury. My case was one of several presented to the jury, but I was the only owner to get more than the state had offered.

Helpful Information in the Tax Records

Another source of basic data on real estate values is the local tax assessor's office or treasurer's office. Assessment records show the value on which taxes are based. The tax rolls show the amount of taxes and the identity of persons to whom the tax bills are sent (usually, though not always, the owners). These records ordinarily are kept at municipal or township offices, but in some states they may be at the county treasurer's or county auditor's office.

Tax assessment records give you at least one appraisal for the land you're considering and any comparables. Sometimes these records will reflect both the estimated market value and the value for tax purposes, which often differ. If the records show only the value for tax purposes, you need to learn from tax officials the relationship of this value to estimated market value. Often the value for tax purposes is less than estimated market value. You need to find out the ratio set by state or local law, or followed by local custom. Michigan, for instance, requires that taxable value be 50 percent of market value. In Ohio, it's 35 percent—which means a property assessed at $7,000 for taxes was estimated to be worth $20,000 on the market. If you know the percentage, you can calculate the market value as estimated by the tax assessor by using this formula:

Assessed Value ÷ Percentage

Calculating Value from the Tax Rolls

It is possible to calculate the assessed value for tax purposes from a property's tax bill if for any reasons the assessment records are not accessible. For this, you need to know the local tax rate, so you can use this formula:

Taxes ÷ Tax Rate

Here's an example. Let's say the annual taxes are $266 and the rate is 47.5 mills (meaning $47.50 per $1,000 of assessed value, or .0475 times the assessed value). Divide $266 by .0475 to get the assessed value:

$$
\begin{array}{r}
5600 \\
.0475\overline{)266.0000} \\
237\ 5 \\
\hline
28\ 50 \\
28\ 50 \\
\hline
\end{array}
$$

The assessed value is $5,600. If assessed value is supposed to be 35 percent of market value, you now divide $5,600 by .35 to get the market value as estimated by the tax assessor:

$$
\begin{array}{r}
160\ 00 \\
.35\overline{)5,600.00} \\
3\ 5 \\
\hline
2\ 10 \\
2\ 10 \\
\hline
\end{array}
$$

The estimated market value is $16,000, as calculated from the amount of annual taxes paid.

Since different places have different tax procedures, be sure you know all the facts and ratios needed to make accurate calculations. In Ohio, for instance, the total property tax for all local units of government—county, city, schools and special assessment districts—is figured for the entire year, then split into two equal semiannual payments. When calculating in this circumstance, it's necessary to use the total annual tax, not just one of the semiannual bills. Michigan does it differently, billing for school taxes at one time of the year, and other taxes at another. You must adapt your calculations to your state and local tax system.

A Couple of Hitches and How to Adjust for Them

Using assessment records and tax rolls in this manner has two catches, however. These are:

1. Tax assessment values are not always up to date; and
2. They represent only one judgment—that of the tax assessor, one of his employees, or a tax appraisal firm retained by the local government.

It's hard to know how accurate, thorough, or diligent the evaluation was, or how it would compare with the estimates of other appraisers. In some locales, tax assessors tend to value all property on the low side; in others, it's the opposite. Or an assessor may be high on some types of land and low on others. Local politics frequently influences tax assessments. Studies have shown that local tax assessing procedures are often afflicted by corruption and other abuses as well as sloppiness. Vulnerability to abuse and the inexactness of appraisal methods constitute a quicksand of unreliability and inequity beneath America's property tax system. This may eventually force abandonment or overhaul of the tax system.

You may be able to learn how recently an assessment was made and what the assessor's tendencies are by asking, but the other matters are not so easy to pin down. Nevertheless, the tax assessor's appraisal is useful information to be weighed along with other facts. As a rule, tax assessments tend to be on the low side, if for no other reason than that they're usually not updated yearly to keep up with price increases—though officials in a few areas are beginning to make annual increases based on such general factors as cost-of-living rises and price indexes. So you can use the assessor's estimate to your advantage in the price bargaining.

Watching Out for Hidden Costs

Tax records can serve the additional purpose of alerting you to hidden costs or unseen factors affecting value. Low taxes constitute one of the reasons why raw land is a good investment for the nonrich. But if taxes seem high, it may mean something is askew. It might mean the price is lower than true value, which could indicate you've found a terrific bargain. On the other hand, it might mean the value used to be higher and something has happened to lower it's worth and attractiveness—such as a change in the area's development trends or construction of a freeway that interfered with convenient access. It's important to investigate further, first by asking tax officials.

If it turns out just to be a high tax rate in the area, you still must consider that it will be an annual expense as long as you own the land.

Tax records should also show whether there are any special assessments in effect for water mains, sewer lines, road improvements or other public facilities that affect the cost of ownership. Information on any new special assessments expected in the future should be obtained from tax officials or the local road, health, water, engineering and planning agencies while you're checking public services and utilities available to the land.

The possibility of such hidden costs is greater in suburban areas than in vacation land, where the availability of utilities may be of more concern. However, in both situations, the lack of such facilities means the landowner someday will have to pay his share for constructing them. One reason why undeveloped land is cheaper is that such costs have yet to be incurred. However, such improvements usually increase the land's value by more than their cost. Whether that's likely to be true in a particular case is a matter for careful evaluation.

Among other potential hidden costs are expensive changes that might be needed in terrain, condition, access, or other aspect in order to make high-value use feasible. These can adversely affect the price you get when you sell.

One of Many Pitfalls in Development Projects

Hidden costs are among the reasons why buying land in a development project should be avoided. Lot owners, according to the fine print in the purchase contract, may be obligated to pay for a water supply system, be subject to assessment for road maintenance, or be required to pay a big tap-in fee before connecting to the water or sewer lines. Even if such extra charges apply only to those who build on their lots and you plan to resell rather than build, the sale price you can get may be reduced by the buyer's need to consider the additional expense. Also, taxes are higher on developed land.

At one project in Pennsylvania, for instance, the "property report" required by law did mention that buyers might have to pay as much as $3,500 for a sewage disposal plant in addition to $7,000 per lot, but salesmen tried to divert attention from the report by telling prospective buyers that they didn't have to read it. Many sales brochures and property statements by development projects describe impressive plans for water systems and other facilities without making it clear whether buyers will have to pay for them later.

Why There's Little Profit Left in Developed Land

You can rarely get a good price on land in a development project. The price includes all the many development costs, including planning, surveying, engineering, roads, utilities, rezoning, legal fees, advertising, promotion, golf courses and other recreation facilities, administrative overhead, and salesmen's commissions—plus a profit for the developer.

Up to 30 percent of the price often goes to the salesman in commission alone, and another 30 to 35 percent is paid for advertising and promotion. Profits run as high as 35 percent. Developers sell land for 10, 20 and 30 times more than they paid for it. I've seen ¼-acre lots (no bigger than city lots) in a vacation-land development advertised for $5,995 and up—meaning a price of $36,000 an acre.

The lots may someday be in such furious demand that the $36,000-an-acre investment shoots up to $72,000 an acre and you make a killing. But that's gambling, not investing. The big value leap that occurs with usage change is already past; and there's unlikely to be another usage change for a long time. Development for a particular use with the appropriate zoning and approval by local authorities locks in that use for the foreseeable future. It's not the same as premature zoning that leaves lots of room for price increases and later zoning changes.

A Revealing Discussion on "Pre-Development" Land

Your chances for profit are always far better in undeveloped land that's on the verge of being in demand for development. This is sometimes known as *pre-development land*.

I once had an opportunity to discuss with a representative of a vacation-land development the merits of buying land in his project compared to investing in raw land outside any development.

"You must be aware," he said, "that pre-development does not reflect the actual resale value of the lot. There is nothing there right now. There will be. So the price that you buy it at will not be the price you sell it at. Let's say you buy a $2,000 lot. One year from now, that $2,000 lot will be worth around $3,100, $3,300, or somewhere in that vicinity." He wanted me to think that buying land in the project early was the same as buying pre-development land.

"Yeah," I said, "but with $2,000 I can buy 10 acres of undeveloped land."

"But you wouldn't make $3,100."

"It would probably increase more than that."

"Pure acreage doesn't increase as fast as pre-development," he said. "Not in a year's time."

He was right in theory; the catch was that what he was selling was not true pre-development land. He also admitted that the lots couldn't continue forever to increase by 50 percent every year.

Finally he said, "I tend to agree with you. I would buy 10 acres, rather than one acre." But, he added, "I don't see where you're going to get 10 acres for $2,000."

His "pre-development" land was, of course, partially developed land with most of the improvements yet to be made—meaning I would have had little but promises for $2,000 an acre. If I had bought any of that land, the developer would have made the big profit, not I. That's not the right idea at all. True pre-development land is outside development projects, land that you get to before the developer, while you can still get a low price.

8

TRAPS
TO STAY OUT OF

Two couples from Dearborn, Mich., drove into a vacation land development called Cedar Hedge Lake near Traverse City in northern Michigan. The sales office was abuzz with people eating free hot dogs and donuts, and marking the lots they had bought on a big wall map.

A salesman showed the Dearborn couples around part of the development where some cottages were under construction. He spoke glowingly about the fishing in the lake, the sunbathing on the sandy beaches, and the snowmobiling in the winter. He said a state legislator was among the lot owners and there weren't many lots left because they were selling like hot cakes.

"It was attractive property," one of the wives said later. "The golf course was right on the corner as you went in. There was a little canal running into the lake. They said they'd clean out the canal for us and cut down the trees."

They asked if they could show the contract to a lawyer before buying. The salesman said the special price of $2,000 per lot was available only that day, and the lots would probably be gone by the time they got back, anyway. Each couple put a deposit on two lots. Later, they paid the rest of the price and asked for deeds to their lots.

The lots they bought, however, were not among those they had seen. While waiting for their deeds, they went back to the development and discovered the "canal" was just a ditch in their part of the development and their lots were covered with swampy water. They also learned the lots were too small for any structure except a trailer or a tent. Since they had not yet received their deeds, they tried to get a refund. That's when they began to discover the painful truth.

Selling Land They Don't Own

The reason they hadn't received their deeds was that the developer had no power to execute the deeds. He did not own the land. All the two couples actually got for their money was an option that was to turn into a purchase contract when the developer secured approval from local authorities for his plat. But, as it turned out, even if he had submitted a plat and obtained approval (which hadn't been done), he still could not have delivered the deeds because he had not yet completed payment on his own contract to buy the land.

The practice by developers of selling land they don't yet own—through such devices as options, purchase contracts and "agreements for deeds" —became so widespread in Michigan in recent years that state attorney general Frank Kelley went to court to stop it. Kelley filed suit, in fact, against the Cedar Hedge Lake developer, alleging misrepresentation, unethical conduct and illegal practices. New legislation was drafted to protect consumers.

An elderly couple bought a lot in a big development near Michigan's Houghton Lake resort area and built a $35,000 home. Two years later, they were served with a foreclosure notice, even though they had paid in full. They thought they had bought land, but all they had was a worthless piece of paper, an agreement the developer couldn't honor because he hadn't completed his own purchase of the land. The true owner was foreclosing because the developer had defaulted on his payments.

Buyers who lost money in the exorbitantly priced Hiawatha East project in Michigan's Upper Peninsula received only an "Agreement for Deed" when they paid their money. This impressive-looking document promised to deliver a deed and title insurance "upon completion of all payments." Salesmen encouraged buyers not to pay the full price in cash. The reason for this, it was disclosed later, was that the developer didn't own the land. The buyers lost their money when the developer went out of business. The development firm owned no land or other assets for buyers and creditors to seize, and there was no money for refunds. A suburban businessman who paid $11,200, sight unseen, for two 10.1-acre lots lost it all. Another man lost $40,000.

How the Scheme Was Supposed to Work

What these developers were trying to do was develop and sell land with little or no investment of their own, using the cash coming in from sales to complete their purchase of the land, cover expenses, and do enough development work to keep sales going.

"They want to develop, but they don't have any money," said Michigan

Health Department engineer Harold Baar. "If he can sell the first ten lots, then he has the money to build a road. And pretty soon he can hire a surveyor and an engineer." It's a new way, Baar said, "to operate on other people's money."

If sales keep booming, it can work. But, it often doesn't. Sales slow down and everything collapses. In the resultant defaults or bankruptcies, it's the buyer who gets hurt the most. This happens not only with well-intentioned developers who try to pull off an enterprise on a shoestring, but also with out-and-out crooks. "There are some," said Baar, "who apparently have no intention of platting or do so only when it becomes absolutely necessary." There have also been cases in which developers under pressure to deliver deeds have produced phony documents or deeds that falsely purport to convey title.

Other Little Hooks to Avoid

This is just one of the pitfalls you risk if you buy a lot in a development, in addition to high price and the danger of hidden costs. Many developers do not engage in unethical tactics, but you need to be a clairvoyant and a genius to tell who is honest and who isn't. Besides, there are numerous problems and perils even in dealing with reputable developers, especially when a time payment contract is involved. Bigness is no reliable guide, either, since some of the big development corporations have been caught using shady methods, too.

The company that's developed the huge Pocono Country Place project in Pennsylvania has required buyers to sign a note that gives the developer a lien not only against the lot being purchased, but also against any other real estate the buyer owns in Pennsylvania. Some installment sale contracts have fine print that says you can't set foot on the land until you make all the payments. There also are some that give the developer the right to sell your lot to someone else and keep all the money you've already paid if you miss a payment by more than 10 or 15 days.

Promises That Aren't Kept and Things That Go Wrong

If these aren't enough reasons to convince you not to buy land in a development project for investment purposes, here are some more:

1. Clubhouses, golf courses, boat marinas, riding stables and other promised facilities that never get built.

2. Lakes, rivers and canals that never get cleared. Tree stumps, underbrush and debris that never get removed. Uncrowded beaches that aren't uncrowded. Recreation areas that can't be used because of unsanitary conditions or uncomfortable terrain.

3. Loss of the lot if you don't build on it within a certain time.

4. Inability to build on a lot or otherwise use it because no water supply or utilities are available, or because health authorities limit the number of septic tanks that may be installed in the area due to high ground water or clay soil. Failure of developers to keep promises to build a water supply system or sewage disposal system.

5. No access to your lot because roads aren't built.

6. Empty guarantees of environmental controls, pure water and scenic preservation, with development for maximum density instead.

7. Unclear boundaries due to inadequate survey work.

8. Nearby conditions that detract from value, such as a passel of delapidated shacks, a trash dump or a rifle range.

9. Developer's disregard for assurance he gave that he'd buy your lot back at the same price or help you sell it if you don't like it; he's got enough competition without helping you sell yours.

White Sand Beaches, Blue Waters and Paradise Lost

Local, state and federal authorities all across America have been swamped with complaints in recent years from people who bought land in development projects only to discover later that the white sand beaches and blue waters they bought were a Florida swamp, or their "paradise in the woods" was an inaccessible patch of ravines. Authorities have taken action against many promoters and developers, including some of the big firms, for deceptive practices and outright fraud.

The Federal Trade Commission in 1974 forced GAC Corp., a giant land company, to refund $17 million to buyers victimized by deceptive advertising in ten projects, nine in Florida and one in Arizona. Lake Havasu Estates, an Arizona land sales firm connected with the famous Lake Havasu City developers who brought the London Bridge to America to be an attraction gimmick, was indicted for fraud and misrepresentation in 1973. That same year California got a court order to stop a Cincinnati firm from selling near-worthless land with a mail order "free gift" pitch. Boise Cascade was ordered by a California jury to pay $543,321 damages to two men who alleged misrepresentation. New York's state attorney general won a court judgment of $388,000 restitution to buyers against a Florida land company named Corporation of Americas Ltd. The U.S. Postal Inspection Service obtained federal indictments against four corporations for trickery, fraudulent pretenses, and high pressure tactics in a Maine land project where lots weren't suitable for homesites because of steep slopes.

Accelerating Action by Aroused Authorities

While more and more states are moving to toughen controls on land development and protect consumers against deception, federal authorities have used two recently enacted laws to act against unscrupulous developers and set up rules to give buyers more protection, especially in requiring developers to make full disclosure of all information about the land they are selling.

Since it was set up in 1969 under the Interstate Land Sales Full Disclosure Act, the Office of Interstate Land Sales Registration in the U.S. Department of Housing and Urban Development has required developers to register full disclosure when more than 50 lots are involved, and to provide prospective buyers with a detailed property report or offering statement.

This report or statement is required to contain facts about such aspects as road distances to nearby communities, financial terms, refund policies, protection in case of the developer's or seller's default, availability of facilities and utilities, and the developer's obligation on such matters as a water supply system. If a buyer does not receive such a report before he signs a purchase contract, he can void the deal. If he gets the report less than 48 hours prior to signing, he can cancel within 48 hours afterward.

Besides putting out pamphlets to tell consumers how to protect themselves, the Interstate Land Sales office can take action to enforce the disclosure and registration requirements. So far it has issued more than 275 suspension orders against developers for noncompliance. It has secured refunds to land purchasers of more than $750,000 from developers who misrepresented their offerings, and more than $5 million from developers of unregistered subdivisions. There have been eight indictments and three convictions for violations as a result of the office's enforcement efforts. "Often we are able to achieve compliance without suspending sales," says Deputy Administrator John R. McDowell.

"Judging from the number of inquiries now received," McDowell said in 1974, "particularly from people who are inquiring before they buy the land, and from the cooperation we now receive from most developers, it appears that our efforts have been successful." McDowell said more protection for consumers has been provided by new regulations on land development advertising, including a ban on the use of the word, "investment."

The other important federal law is the Truth in Lending Act that gives buyers 72 hours to cancel an installment purchase contract after signing it.

Loopholes and Weaknesses in the Laws

Despite all the revelations about deceptive and fraudulent practices, and despite new laws, stiffer regulations and action by government to protect buyers, millions of Americans still get cheated on overpriced bits of low-grade land and there are still many dangers in buying development project land.

One reason is that the laws aren't very effective. The Interstate Land Sales Full Disclosure Act applies only to interstate sales, and not to developers operating only in one state. Some states deal sternly only with out-of-state land promoters, but not with developments in their own states. Out-of-state firms can circumvent such state laws by setting up separate subsidiaries in each state. Many states have no effective laws at all, and there's no uniformity from state to state. California's relatively tough laws, for instance, merely drive some developers into other states.

Clever developers use sly tricks to thwart the law. Some get buyers to sign a statement that they received and read the property report even though they didn't actually get one. Salesmen try to discourage buyers from reading the report. Some contracts include a waiver of the right to cancel during the 48-hour "cooling off period"; if you sign it, you can't cancel. A particularly sneaky gimmick is a contract provision in which you acknowledge you don't intend to use the property as your principal residence. If it's vacation land, you might think there's no harm in signing that. But, what that really is is a waiver of your right to cancel within 72 hours under the Truth in Lending Act, since a loophole in that law exempts land that the buyer does not intend to use for his principal residence.

Authorities do not have enough money or manpower to enforce the laws effectively. Most state agencies admit they are too understaffed to keep up with complaints and investigate all the suspected cases of misrepresentation and fraud.

Costly Boomerang Effects

Some of the new laws and regulations have a kind of backfire effect. Buyers think they're automatically protected when they're not, causing them to be careless. Developers use the illusion of protection to practice still more deception. They make a big point of the fact that their development is registered with a state or federal agency, implying that the agency has given their development a government stamp of approval when that's not the case at all.

Complying with government regulations also has the effect of raising the developer's expenses, since he must publish a detailed property report, fill out forms, and get additional legal advice. These expenses are passed on to buyers in the form of higher prices.

The Best Protection Is Self-Protection

No matter what steps the government takes, you still have to watch for yourself what you're doing. The government can only do so much toward protecting a person from his own gullibility. One thing on which most authorities agree is that it's up to you to protect yourself. It's you who must resist the pressures, blandishments and temptations to "get in on the land boom" in the wrong place; no one can do it for you.

If you do buy in a development subdivision, anyway, despite the pitfalls and the poor profit potential, be sure to read the property report or prospectus carefully. Have your attorney read it, too. Don't sign anything before you see the land and have a thorough understanding of all the facts.

If a development salesman is reluctant to give you the property report or tries to convince you it's not important, be suspicious. Check with the Interstate Land Sales Registration Office in Washington (U.S. Department of Urban Development, Washington, D.C. 20411), state and local consumer protection agencies, and local prosecutors. Find out how many others have complained.

Above all, never sign away your right to cancel. Make sure there's no cancellation waiver before you sign.

The Foolproof Way Not to Become a Developer's Victim

The best way to avoid buying high-priced land in a development project is not to visit any and not to submit yourself to their diabolical sales techniques and pressures. In other words, don't deal with them at all. Buying land in a development project is more like a donation than an investment.

If you don't make any contact with development sales operations, you don't have to figure out who's honest and who isn't. Many big developers complain that a few borderline operators and crooks give the industry an undeserved bad image. Some government officials admit, too, that "bad developers" hurt the reputation of "good developers" because it's difficult for the public to know the difference. But the good developers aren't doing anything about the bad developers except complain. The foolproof way to make sure you don't deal with a bad one is not to deal with any.

Besides, even when buying from an ethical and legitimate developer, you're still not getting a good deal for investment and profit purposes.

Resisting the High-Pressure Hustlers

Avoiding the development project promoters, however, can sometimes be easier said than done. Ingeniously crafted enticements designed to exploit the weaknesses of human nature arrive unsolicited in the mail and on the phone. Land hustlers have devised a number of devilish tactics to get you to make some kind of commitment—even if only a $5 "refundable" deposit—before you see what you're buying or after just one brief look. A refundable deposit compels you to visit the land before you can get it back, and that means submitting yourself to fiendish pressure in a captive situation.

Most development project sales strategy is aimed at getting the buyer to make the first commitment, however small. That puts him on the hook. Many use "boiler room" banks of telephone girls who set up appointments for high-powered salesmen or invite you to a "free" steak dinner that turns out to be a pressure-cooker sales presentation. Some have phony "account executives" call you up and read from a script that's psychologically calculated to get you to mail in a $5 or $25 deposit to "hold" a lot for you "before the price goes up" until you can get to the development and see the land. Invitations to "free" trips to Florida and Arizona developments arrive in the mail. So do offers of "free" gifts or discounts if you show up at developments closer to home to see what they have. The idea is to make that first commitment easy to make and hard to turn down.

If you make an appointment, accept the dinner invitation, go on the "free" trip, make any kind of deposit, sign any agreement to visit the project, or do anything that compels you to submit yourself to the high pressure sales tactics awaiting you at the development, you have taken the bait. Salesmen are taught the importance of getting a prospect to make such a commitment, because that usually leads to a sale. Chances are that if you don't bite the first time, you won't be back. It's up to you not to bite that first time, unless a high-priced lot in a project is what you want, or you need the free dinner and are confident of your stamina and ability in resisting high-pressure tactics.

An Example of How Not to Resist

Being interested in land can sometimes make one more attentive to land promotion pitches than he should be. One of my daughters once received a form letter saying she had won a free trip to Florida and "the fabulous Walt Disney World." It turned out to be part of a promotion scheme to sell lots in a Florida land project. The "free" trip actually included only hotel accommodations for two adults for three nights and two adult tickets to Disney World. There would be a land sales presentation, but no obligation to attend. To register for the free trip, one had to pay a $19.80 "service fee." There was also a free camera.

My daughter was quite excited, which, of course, was part of the hustle. Because of that, because I'm interested in land but felt I could resist buying, and because there was at least an $8 camera to be obtained, I paid the $19.80.

We never did make the trip and didn't get the $19.80 back, either. I kept asking myself how I could fall for such an obvious trick. It showed how important it is never to relax your guard. Just when you think you're so knowledgeable and sophisticated that no one can fool you, zap! They get you.

The Painful Costs of "Free" Trips

It can be worse, though, to actually go on the trip, especially if you use any transportation except your own automobile. If you have your car, you can get in and drive away if the pressure tactics get too obnoxious. But if you go by plane or chartered bus, you can't get away so easily. One trick is to make you feel obligated to buy something because you've already received so much "free."

Another trick is to show you a map with all the lots marked "sold" except for a few. At one northern Michigan land project, salesmen took prospects around in a car with a two-way radio on which a voice would keep reporting that another lot was sold. The idea, of course, is to make buyers anxious to buy land that's so desirable it's selling faster than ice water in a desert.

I know a salesman who quit working for a development firm because the prospects he lined up to take bus trips to one of its projects came back angry at him for leading them into excruciating pressure. He took one of the bus trips, himself, to see what they meant. "I just couldn't send anybody else up there to be put under that enormous pressure," he told me. "I didn't realize what they were doing. They put people in a room and wouldn't let them out until they signed."

The purpose of pressuring you over the phone or at a free dinner to make a deposit that's refundable after you see the land is as fair as it's supposed to seem. Not at all. The purpose is to get you to the project site so you can be pressured more efficiently. The same is true of free gifts you can get only by visiting the development project.

The way to avoid such trips and pressures is not to go to free dinners or take free trips in the first place. Don't respond to mail invitations, don't talk to salesmen, hang up on telephone solicitations, and don't visit development projects. Look for land investments elsewhere.

The Proper Application of Your Profit Motive

Many land hustlers aim their pitch at your profit motive. They say things like, "Get in on the ground floor of the land boom," "Land is the best place to invest for profit," and "There's big money in land from appreciation in value." Some of it sounds similar to what this book is saying, but there's a big difference. With developers, it's just a sales pitch to make profits for them, not you. The ground floor is already gone.

What makes the pitch so potent is that it's half true. You can make big profits in land. But not in the developed land they're selling. The price is high, since it includes the costs of all those free trips and steak dinners, and most of the profit is already eaten up. The parcels are also too small for much further appreciation. Don't let developers exploit your profit motive for their profit. The proper use of profit motive is for your profit.

Pitfalls and Traps in Other Places, Too

Though development projects are the most visible, most obvious traps to avoid, they're by no means the only ones. You can also encounter many of the same pitfalls—overpricing, hidden costs, low profit potential, high pressure tactics, misrepresentation, concealed flaws, uncertain ownership, deception, and unkept promises—with other sellers.

Individual owners, realty firms and other investors who buy and sell land may not show you a film at a "free" dinner, but they may practice plenty of other wiles that inveigle people into buying land they probably shouldn't buy. Their advertising can be as misleading as any that's put out by project promoters. It's normal, after all, for sellers to describe their land in the most favorable terms. It's up to you to discover the drawbacks. You don't even have as many laws to help you.

If an ad or sales pitch says there are five beautiful, fish-filled lakes within walking distance, the area is surrounded with new resorts under construction, the woods abound with game, a new shopping center is planned for half a mile down the road, or land values are rising 20 percent every year, don't just accept it on faith. Check it out yourself.

You should be wary, for example, of 5-acre and 10-acre parcels of vacation land that are not, strictly speaking, in a development project or otherwise developed. These often have been carved out of larger tracts, but without any development improvements like new roads or utilities. Though not priced as high as development project lots, they are still relatively high. It's no longer a groundfloor situation, since the quickest, easiest, biggest profits go to the seller who carved them up. You probably would still make some profit, since there is sure to be further appreciation, but such parcels may not be easy to resell and they're usually difficult to subdivide further. You do much better if you're the one who buys the larger tracts and carves them up into 5-acre and 10-acre pieces for resale.

Never forget the basic rule of making your own decisions and basing them on facts, not on someone else's sales pitch, promises or predictions. Never make a decision while under pressure and never be in a hurry.

Don't be unduly swayed by the ease of credit buying. Don't let talk about "low down payment" and "easy monthly payments"—one of the high-pressure land hustler's most powerful weapons—divert you from the really important facts like location and price. But, this is not to say that you shouldn't buy on a credit arrangement with a low down payment. That, in fact, is the way you should buy, once you have the right location and price. Installment buying is the secret of maximizing and multiplying your profits through the tactic of leverage.

9

HOW TO MULTIPLY AND PYRAMID YOUR PROFITS

When I sold those 80 acres of land for a net price of $10,000 and made a profit of $6,000, it appeared that I had gained a return of 150 percent on a $4,000 investment.

That would have amounted to an average annual return of 37.5 percent over the four years I had the land—a fabulous rate of profit compared to the 12 to 15 percent per year that's usually considered highly attractive in investments.

However, appearances can be misleading. Actually, I did even better than 150 percent because I didn't have $4,000 invested. My total investment over the four years, including a $200 down payment and the amount of monthly payments applied to the land purchase, was only about $3,025.

When I sold the land, I still owed $975 on my own purchase contract. After I paid that $975 from the $10,000 I received, I had $9,025 left. Since I had invested $3,025, my profit was still $6,000. But that represented a return of 198.3 percent on $3,025 instead of 150 percent—and 49.6 percent per year instead of only 37.5 percent.

Since the $3,025 had not been invested all at once, but over a period of four years, the true profit rate was even greater than 198.3 percent. To calculate it precisely, I'd have to prorate the profit according to the portion of each monthly payment that was applied to the principal. Then I could figure the profit rate separately for each month and determine the average rate for the year. I must admit that I have never gotten around to doing that.

Heftier Profit for Each Dollar

This is a modest example of the tremendous financial leverage you get when you buy on a land contract or other installment arrangement with a small down payment. You get a lot of result from a little input. The actual profit ends up roughly the same, but you need less money to get it because you invest only a fraction of the price. This means, in turn, that you can make much bigger profits with whatever amount you have to invest by using the leverage power of credit buying.

In the case of my 80 acres, the total amount invested—$3,025—was not a great deal less than the $4,000 purchase price. But it was enough to pry up the profit percentage from 37.5 percent per year to 49.6 percent, and I had four years to come up with the $3,025.

Multiplier Effect vs. Interest Costs

If you're thinking that's not the whole story because you have to pay interest when you buy on credit, you're right. The interest does reduce the profit. But if you buy right, the power of leverage to multiply profits far outweighs the interest cost.

Let's examine closely the case of my 80 acres, in which I paid interest costs and property taxes totaling $890 over four years before I sold the land. (Taxes are included in order to get the total picture, even though property taxes must be paid regardless of whether you pay cash or buy on time.)

That $890 would seem to reduce the profit to $5,110. However, that's not the entire story, either, since interest and property taxes are deductible on the federal income tax. Using my average income tax rate of about 20 percent during those four years, I would have saved $178 on income tax. My actual cost for interest and property taxes was $712:

Total taxes and interest	$890
Income tax saved	178
Net cost, taxes and interest	$712

Deducting that cost of $712 from my $6,000 profit left me a more accurate profit figure of $5,288:

Gross profit	$6,000
Net cost, taxes and interest	712
Net profit	$5,288

On my investment of $3,025, this represents a return of 175 percent—or 43.75 percent per year:

$$
\begin{array}{r}
174.8 \\
\hline
3{,}025\,/5{,}288 \\
3{,}025 \\
\hline
2\ 2630 \\
2\ 1175 \\
\hline
14550 \\
12100 \\
\hline
2450\ 0 \\
2420\ 0 \\
\hline
\end{array}
$$

This is still better than 150 percent for four years and 37.5 percent per year. And, again, I didn't have to invest that $3,025 all at one time in the beginning; I had four years to do it.

The Most Valuable Secret of All

The main value of installment plan leverage in my 80-acre deal was not so much in the smaller total investment as in the ability to get the land in the first place with only $200 in cash. The opportunity to get $4,000 worth of land with only $200 in cash, and then make the rest of the investment bit by bit with monthly payments I could handle, was the real secret to being able to make a $5,288 profit.

There was no way I could have made the purchase at all if I had needed to put up the entire $4,000, or even half that much, to swing the deal in the beginning.

A Similar Case of Astronomical Percentages

A more spectacular example is the 1.7-acre parcel I bought north of Detroit in expectation of having a gasoline station site next to a freeway interchange. The purchase price was $9,000, but I paid only $1,000 down and $80 a month. When the Michigan highway department condemned most of it and paid me $11,000, I had invested only $2,865 over four years. I paid off my contract from the $11,000, recovered my $2,865 investment, and made an apparent profit of $2,000.

However, it cost me $666 for an appraiser and attorney in the condemnation suit. This reduced the apparent profit from $2,000 to $1,334.

In addition, I had paid $1,725 in property taxes and interest, affecting the profit as follows:

Total taxes and interest	$1,725
Income tax saved (at 20%)	345
Net cost, taxes and interest	$1,380
Gross profit	$1,334
Net cost, taxes and interest	1,380
Net loss	$(46)

I apparently was left with a $46 loss, except for one thing. I still have .7 acre left and it's worth up to $60,000 or more. My current investment in that land is only that $46 I lost. I've not had to make any more payments or pay any further interest, just pay the taxes, which have amounted to a total of about $1,000.

If I sold that remaining piece of land in 1976, say, for $60,000, and deducted the tax expense—of about $1,000 after subtracting the income tax savings—the net profit would be $58,954.

On an investment of $46, this would be a mind-boggling return of 128,160 percent, or an average of 16,020 percent per year for the eight years since the condemnation in 1968.

A Fantastic Profit No Matter How You Figure It

If that's just too astounding to believe, figure the $1,000 in property taxes as part of the investment instead as an expense, making the investment $1,046. (Though technically the tax cost is an expense rather than a capital investment, the $1,046 figure does represent the total cash put into the land one way or another.)

On this basis, the profit percentage would only be 5,636 percent, or 704.5 percent per year.

To figure the profit rate as low as possible, I could use as the investment figure the total of everything I ever put into the land, including all taxes and interest and even the original investment despite the fact that I got that back from the state highway department. The figures would look like this:

Proceeds from 1976 sale		$60,000
Original investment recovered		2,865
Profit at condemnation		1,334
Total receipts		$64,199
Less costs		
Investment	$2,865	
Pre-1968 tax & interest cost (adjusted for income tax savings)	1,380	
Taxes since 1968 (adjusted)	1,000	
Total	$5,245	$ 5,245
Net profit		$58,954

The profit is the same, but calculating the percentage of return on the $5,245 total cost figure as the investment, the rate is down to 1,124 percent—or 93.7 percent per year for the 12 years since the original purchase.

Here's how the calculation looks:

$$
\begin{array}{r}
11.24 \\
5{,}245\,\overline{)58{,}954} \\
52\ 45 \\
\overline{6\ 504} \\
5\ 245 \\
\overline{1\ 259\ 0} \\
1\ 049\ 0 \\
\overline{210\ 00} \\
\underline{209\ 80}
\end{array}
$$

No matter how you figure it, the profit you can make with installment buying leverage is enormous. The return would be great in this case even if I had paid the $9,000 full price in cash in the beginning, of course, since my investment after the state paid me $11,000 was $46 regardless of how much I originally put into the deal. But I didn't have $9,000 in the beginning. The most I could scrape together was $1,000. If I hadn't been able to make the purchase on a land contract with $1,000 down, there would have been no deal and my profit would be zero.

Another Set of Sky-High Profit Figures

Another example is the 600 feet of frontage I bought on Pike Lake in Michigan's Upper Peninsula. The price was $20,000, but I paid $2,500 down on a land contract and agreed to pay $120 a month, with interest at 7 percent per year.

If I had sold it in June of 1975, three years after the purchase, I would have had about $3,300 invested by then, and about $3,000 in interest and tax costs (after subtracting the federal income tax saved at 20 percent). If I got $75 a foot for the land, a total of $45,000, my profit would be as follows:

Gross proceeds	$45,000
Less original cost	20,000
($3,300 invested plus amount still owed)	——
Gross profit	$25,000
Less tax & interest cost	3,000
Net profit	$22,000

On the investment of $3,300, this would be a return of 666.67 percent over three years—222.33 percent per year.

The profit would be slightly higher—$22,000 plus $2,700 in interest costs I wouldn't have had—if I had paid $20,000 cash. But the $24,700 profit would have been a return of only 123.5 percent on the $20,000 investment, or only 41.2 percent per year.

Buying on contract, I needed to put up only $2,500 at first, plus another $800 and taxes and interest of $3,000—a total paid out of $6,300—to make $22,000. Otherwise, I would have had to put up $20,000 that I didn't have.

Why Not to Pay Cash Even If You Can

Actually, if I had had the $20,000 in cash, it would have been poor technique to put it all into the full price of one piece of land, anyway. Even when you have plenty of cash, you should still use the leverage of installment plan buying to multiply, maximize and pyramid your profits.

For example, $20,000 could be used to make down payments of $2,500 on eight different properties. If each were to make $10,000 in four years, you'd have $80,000 in profits instead of one profit of only $10,000. If eight monthly payments are too many, try just four, investing $10,000 in down payments and keeping the other $10,000 to help make payments and have a reserve fund. You'd still make $40,000 instead of $10,000. Even after you deduct your interest costs, you're still making a lot more money.

The Key to Leverage—Other People's Money

This kind of financial leverage, even more so than the leverage of low price, is the basic secret of truly big profits in land. It is a method of operating on, or using, other people's money to make profits for yourself. It's the same as borrowing and making a greater return on the borrowed money than it costs you to borrow it.

Big investors, from wealthy individuals to giant corporations, work mostly on other people's money most of the time—borrowed money or invested capital from the purchasers of stock. So do land developers, both big and small, real estate firms, and all sorts of other business enterprises, from mining and manufacturing to the popcorn stand in the shopping mall. Construction of homes, stores, factories, office towers and other structures is almost always done on borrowed funds.

Operating and making a profit on other people's money, in fact, is a cornerstone of a free enterprise economic system based on the rights of individuals to acquire and own land and other wealth. Investing on the installment plan is a way for the individual who is not already rich to get in on this effective method of becoming rich. And land is about the only low-risk, big-money investment where you can make easy and potent use of financial leverage (though there are some good opportunities in other forms of real estate investment).

When so-called experts advise against buying land on the installment plan, they're either overlooking the leverage factor or they're reluctant to share the secret with you. If they say not to buy at disadvantageous terms, such as a high interest rate or no possession until all payments are completed, they're on solid ground. But just to say not to buy land on credit is to recommend against the very best way you'll ever encounter to make big profits on little money.

The Marvelous Mathematics of Leverage

The arithmetic is simple. If something you own jumps in value from $5 to $10, your value has doubled. But if you control the ownership of the item by paying only $2, you pay the other $3 out of the $10 when you sell. You make a $5 profit on only a $2 investment.

The person to whom you sell the property helps you make the original investment because you defer part of it until you sell. You do not own the property, but you control it with your right to complete a purchase at any time at the original price, even though the value has since increased. You are using another person's money both to maximize your profit and make the investment in the first place.

Whether you pay the full $5 or only $2 down, the profit is $5. But if you pay the entire $5 in the beginning, your profit rate is only 100 percent, and you used $5 to make $5. If you only have $2 in it, your profit rate is 250 percent, and you needed only $2 to make $5.

If you had $5 originally but used it with installment leverage to make a 250 percent profit on the entire $5, your profit would be $12.50 instead of $5. To get an idea of the difference this makes in land investment, make that $5 read $5,000 or $50,000.

A Cash vs. Credit Comparison

Suppose you have a chance to buy 100 acres of well-located land on a paved road not far from a growing vacation area for $100 an acre—a total price of $10,000. After investigating thoroughly, you figure the chances are good that development will spread fast enough to make this land worth $200 an acre in four years or less.

If you have only $2,000, there's no question that you have to buy on credit if you want it, and can get it for 20 percent down. But let's say you have enough cash and you can get the land for only $8,000 if you pay cash. On a land contract, the price stays at $10,000. Which way would bring the most profit?

If you pay $8,000 cash and the land can be sold for $20,000 three years later, your profit would be $12,000, a return of 150 percent on your investment.

On the other hand, if you pay $2,000 down and $80 a month at 8 percent annual interest, it would go like this:

Initial investment		$2,000
First year—total payments	$960	
Approx. total of interest paid at 8% of $8,000 beginning balance	640	
Additional amt. invested	$320	320
Second year—total payments	$960	
Approx. total of interest paid at 8% of beginning balance of $7,680 ($8,000–$320)	610	
Additional amt. invested	$350	350
Third year—total payments	$960	
Approx. total of interest paid at 8% of beginning balance of $7,330 ($7,680–$350)	580	
Additional amt. invested	$380	380
Total invested		$3,050

The profit would be $10,000 ($20,000 minus your purchase price of $10,000, which is the same as the amount invested plus what you'd still owe) less the net cost of interest as shown here:

First year interest	$ 640
Second year interest	610
Third year interest	580
Total	$1,830
Less 20% for income tax savings	370
Net interest cost	$1,460

Leaving out any consideration of property taxes this time since they'd be the same in each case, we figure the net profit to be $8,540.

Gross profit	$10,000
Net interest cost	1,460
Net profit	$ 8,540

This is considerably less than the $12,000 profit you'd make by paying $8,000 cash, but look what happens to your profit rate:

$$
\begin{array}{r}
2.8 \\
\overline{3{,}050\,/8{,}540} \\
6{,}100 \\
\overline{2\ 440\ 0} \\
2\ 440\ 0 \\
\hline
\end{array}
$$

On the investment of $3,050, your return would be 280 percent—almost double the return from a full cash purchase.

Even if you were to figure your interest cost of $1,460 as part of the investment to make the total investment figure $4,510, the $8,540 profit would still represent a return of 189 percent.

In addition, you could invest in more land and get a crack at bigger profits with that $8,000. For example, you could buy two parcels at $2,000 down each and use the other $4,000 to help make payments. After three years, your profits would be $17,080 instead of $8,540 or $12,000. If you could afford to buy more than two pieces that way and make the payments, you'd do even better.

Doubling the Multiplier Effect with Double Leverage

Installment buying is another reason why inexpensive land offers you the best opportunity to make big money in land investment when you have only limited resources. You can get two kinds of leverage at once:

1. Low price.
2. Control of the land with only a portion of the price as a down payment.

You get, in effect, double leverage. You compound the multiplier effect of low-price leverage by using installment leverage, too.

For instance, if you have a choice between buying 50 acres at $100 an acre with $1,000 down on the $5,000 price, or 100 acres at $50 an acre, also with $1,000 down on the same total price, how much difference does it make which one you pick?

Let's say you'd pay $40 a month at 8 percent annual interest in either case and the increase in price is the same—$50 an acre—over the next two years. According to the same type of calculation used in the previous example, you would have about $1,340 invested after two years, in either case. Your net interest cost, using 20 percent as your income tax saving, would be $500 in either case.

The $100-an-acre land would be worth $150 an acre and here's the way your profit would look if you sold it:

Gross proceeds from sale (50 acres)	$7,500
Purchase price (same as total invested plus amount still owed)	5,000
Gross profit	$2,500
Net interest cost	500
Net Profit	$2,000

On your investment of $1,340, this would be a profit of 149 percent—74.5 percent per year.

The $50-an-acre land, however, would be worth twice its purchase price and your profit would be as follows:

Gross proceeds (100 acres @ $100)	$10,000
Purchase price	5,000
Gross profit	$ 5,000
Net interest cost	500
Net profit	$ 4,500

The gross profit is double and the net profit is more than double. On the investment of $1,340, the profit of $4,500 is a return of 336 percent—118 percent per year. This return rate is also more than double what you'd get in the case of the $100-an-acre land.

This difference is not due just to the low-price leverage, but also partly to the installment leverage on top of it. If you paid $5,000 cash, your profit in the $100-an-acre land would still be $2,500 (no interest cost), and in the $50-an-acre land it would still be $5,000. In the first case, the return would be 50 percent and in the second case it would be 100 percent. With regard to both total profit and percentage return, you would do exactly twice as well in the $50 land as in the $100 land, using just low-price leverage.

Using installment leverage in addition, the difference is more than double. This is true in both net profit and rate of return. The net profit of $4,500 in the cheaper land is 2.25 times the net profit of $2,000 in the other. The same is true of the return percentage.

The *maximum rate of return* is obtained by combining both types of leverage. The fastest way to get rich in land is to buy cheap and to buy on credit. Take out a pencil and paper, or one of the new electronic calculators that you can buy inexpensively and use it to figure the effects of leverage quickly and easily. No matter how many examples you try, it always comes out that way.

Increasing the Profit Power of Each Investment Dollar

The ability to accomplish more with each dollar you have to invest is the main benefit of the multiplier effect in leverage. If you have $4,000 left because you paid only $1,000 down on a $5,000 purchase, you can use that $4,000 to buy more low-price, high-leverage land. That way you can control five times as much land (or more if the price is lower) and get five times as much profit (or more if the price increase is greater).

It's better, anyway, to have several investments rather than one, to spread your money among several highly leveraged investments rather than concentrating it all in one. If you have $5,000, you will do better to put $1,000 down on five different parcels worth $5,000 each, than to put $5,000 down on one $25,000 tract.

Not only do you reduce further what little risk may be involved by putting your eggs in more than one basket and applying the insurance principle of spreading the risk, but you usually will find it easier to sell smaller parcels and the price tends to increase faster on smaller parcels. Sometimes a big tract can be split up into smaller pieces for resale at higher prices, but this is not always easy and may be subject to state or local regulations that make it costly.

Unless you want to become a big-money operator or developer and deal in higher stakes and risks, you should stick to medium-size parcels that offer good low-price leverage possibilities. Even after you start making big money, you're still better off reinvesting in several medium-size parcels instead of moving up to big tracts requiring large investments. If you make a $10,000 profit on a deal, for instance, you can build further profits by putting it into $50,000 to $100,000 worth of land on an installment setup. And you can pyramid your profits faster by putting it in four or five parcels, not just one.

After I made $6,000 by selling 80 acres in northern Michigan in 1971, I resolved not to put all of it in one reinvestment. I used $3,000 as down payments on two purchases in the Upper Peninsula—600 feet on Pike Lake and 600 feet on a county road. I figured to use the rest for other small, highly leveraged investments and as a reserve to make sure I could handle the monthly payments.

Pyramiding Leverage on Leverage, Profit on Profit

Pyramiding profits is done by using leverage upon leverage—taking the profit from one leverage deal, investing it again at high leverages, selling again soon, investing the high-leverage profits another time at high leverage, and keeping this up over and over again, turning your land over frequently in highly leveraged deals. This is easiest to do when you have medium-size, low-price parcels that give you a workable balance of leverage and flexibility.

To illustrate: With that $10,000 profit, you buy:

1. A $25,000 parcel with $3,000 down;
2. An $8,000 piece with $2,000 down;
3. An $18,000 tract with $2,500 down; and
4. A $4,000 piece with $500 down.

You have invested $8,000 in $55,000 worth of land and have $2,000 in cash still on hand.

You have a tough time keeping up with payments on all this, so after one year you sell the $25,000 parcel for $28,000. This may not seem like much of a profit, since your interest cost (at 8 percent per year, let's say) is $1,400, which cuts your profit to a net of $1,600. But your investment by then is only about $3,900, so that's still a return of 41 percent in only one year.

As a result of this sale, you now have $6,900 on hand.

Gross proceeds	$28,000
Amount still owed ($25,000 less $3,900 invested— $3,000 down payment plus $900 over one year)	21,100
Net proceeds	$ 6,900

Here's another way of looking at that $6,900:

Investment recovered	$ 3,900
Net profit	1,600
Interest cost recovered (already paid out over the year, and now you have it back even though you deduct it from gross profit to (arrive at your true, or net, profit)	1,400
	$ 6,900

Of that $6,900, you put $1,500 into a $10,000 installment purchase and keep the rest in reserve to make sure you can meet your payment obligations. You now have $40,000 worth of land (instead of $55,000) which you bought with down payments totaling $6,500. In three of the four properties, you also have a year's additional investment and interest costs.

After the second year, you sell the $8,000 piece for $12,000, making $3,250 on a total investment of $2,500 ($2,000 down plus $500 more over two years, with $750 in interest cost). This represents a return of 130 percent in two years. You have $6,500 to reinvest ($12,000 minus the $5,500 you still owed) and you use that as a down payment on $30,000 worth of land.

After the third year, you sell the $18,000 piece for $30,000. By this time, you've invested another $2,000 besides your $2,500 down payment. An interest cost of $2,850 cuts your profit from $12,000 to $9,150. On the $4,500 total investment, however, this is a return of 203 percent over three years. Your net proceeds from the deal, after paying the $13,500 you still owe, are $16,500, which you reinvest in $60,000 worth of land.

After the fourth year, you sell the $4,000 parcel, which you bought with only $500 down, for $12,000. Your investment totals $1,150 and your interest cost has been $800. Your net profit of $7,200 represents a return of 626 percent over four years, or 156.5 percent per year. You have net proceeds of $9,150 to reinvest in, say, $50,000 worth of land.

After the fifth year, you sell for $20,000 the land you bought for $10,000 at the end of the first year (with $1,500 down). You have $3,000 invested by now and an interest cost of $2,000. Your net profit is $8,000, which is a return of 267 percent on the $3,000 investment, or 67 percent per year. You have cash on hand of $13,000.

Bigger Profits from Multiple Turnover

Your situation after five years is this:

$$
\begin{array}{ll}
\text{Profits—\$} & 1,600 \\
& 3,250 \\
& 9,150 \\
& 7,200 \\
& \underline{8,000} \\
& \$\ 29,200
\end{array}
$$

Value of current investments at purchase price—

$$
\begin{array}{l}
\$\ 30,000 \\
60,000 \\
\underline{50,000} \\
\$140,000
\end{array}
$$

And you have $13,000 cash for reinvestment.

This you've accomplished in five years, beginning with only $10,000. You have a turnover rate of one property per year, with each property held for four years. Assuming that values have continued to rise, the actual market value of your holdings is no doubt closer to $200,000 than $140,000.

If you were to sell all your holdings at this point, assuming an average annual increase in value of 15 percent, which is equivalent to a doubling over five years, your profits and cash proceeds would be as follows:

Purchase price	Net profit	Cash on hand
$ 30,000	$10,700	$20,400
60,000	14,500	40,100
50,000	4,900	18,300
$140,000	$30,100	$78,800
Previous totals	29,200	13,000
	$59,300	$91,800

If you had instead put that total down payment of $8,000 into just one piece of land worth $55,000 in the beginning, you would not be so well off. Assuming the land doubled in value over those five years, your gross profit would be $55,000 and your interest cost would be $14,000, leaving you a net profit of $41,000. You'd have cash of $74,000 to invest again.

It's clear that the multiple turnover method does better than the single investment approach. In addition, you derive more advantages from leverage when you continue the frequent buying and selling of medium-size investments instead of cashing them in all at once. In this example, it would have been better to continue the overlapping four-year cycles than to sell all and start over, though it's not necessary to follow quite so precise a schedule.

(In all these comparisons, the figures are approximate and are based on monthly payments equal to one percent of the unpaid balance after the down payment, which is a common practice. For instance, in the $8,000 purchase with $2,000 down, the unpaid balance was $6,000 and the monthly payment $60. An annual interest rate of 8 percent was used in the calculations, with the cost reduced by 20 percent to account for the portion saved on the federal income tax.)

Maximizing the Pyramid Effect with Double Leverage

Pyramiding works by using the profits from one deal as the down payment at high leverage on the next. But the leverage takes a while to gain momentum, just as compounding interest or taking a number to its 10th power. If the rate of land value increase is not high, it takes four or five years. There's not enough appreciation each year to offset the slow-starting effect of pyramiding. But if land values are shooting up fast, such as doubling in two or three years or tripling in three or four years, pyramiding produces dazzling results.

This is why you get the most out of pyramiding with the double leverage of both low-price leverage and credit buying leverage. With a low price per acre (rather than low total price), a 50 percent or 100 percent increase can take place faster. This causes greater profits sooner and accelerates the impact of pyramiding. In the case of the $4,000 purchase with $500 down, here's what happens with pyramiding each year if the value increases 33.3 percent per year:

End of:	Net profit	Cash to reinvest	New purchase
1st year	$ 1,113	$ 1,973	$ 15,000
2nd year	4,200	6,450	48,000
3rd year	13,350	24,000	144,000
4th year	40,000	76,800	600,000

This shows the spectacular effects of pyramiding when land values are rising rapidly in relation to the purchase price, which is most likely to happen when the price is low. The greater the percentage increase in value, the more spectacular the results of pyramiding.

In this example, the cash proceeds were reinvested each year at the same ratio of down payment to purchase price as in the original purchase—namely, 12.5 percent. The lower the down payment percentage, the greater the leverage and the faster the pyramiding.

Solutions to the Payment Problem

The problem, however, is that the payments would be $415 a month during the third year and $1,200 a month in the fourth year, even if you reinvest each year in several parcels. If you can't afford that, you can still do well by reinvesting in such a way as to keep your payments down to, say, less than $60 a month. Here's what happens then:

End of:	Net profit	Cash to reinvest	New purchase
1st year	$1,113	$ 1,973	$ 7,500
2nd year	2,150	4,700	10,500
3rd year	3,130	8,430	14,400
4th year	4,430	13,470	19,200

This compares to a net profit of $7,800 and cash on hand of $9,282 if you hold the land for four years and sell.

Another way to deal with the payment problem is to use only part of the cash proceeds for your next investment, holding back the rest to help you make the payments. You sacrifice some leverage power that way, but that's better than taking on more than you can handle. You need to calculate in each case how much leverage you can afford.

Optimum Balance of Turnover and Leverage

How often you should turn over your land in order to get the most out of the pyramiding effect depends on how fast its value is increasing. If the price is rising at 20 percent per year or less, there's not much difference between selling every year and selling every four or five years, unless you are willing to keep increasing your investment every year in the form of higher monthly payments.

If land valued at $4,000 increases at 15 percent per year, it would be worth $8,000 after five years and you'd make a net profit of $3,000 if you started with a down payment of $500. You'd have cash proceeds of $5,325 to reinvest. If you sold every year and reinvested so as to keep your monthly payments close to $35 a month, the results would be much the same.

You could pyramid total profits for the five years to $11,750 and have cash of $23,475 to reinvest if you sold every year and reinvested at the same high-leverage ratio between down payment and purchase price. But your monthly payments would be up to $500 by the fifth year.

If the annual increase were 20 percent, you'd make a net profit of $3,464 and cash proceeds of $5,434 if you sold after four years. By selling every year and reinvesting to keep your payments under $55 a month, you would make total net profits of $4,420 and have $6,845 to reinvest. This is better, but not by much.

If the annual increase is only 10 percent, it's barely more than the interest rate, yet you'd still profit. At the end of one year in the $4,000-on-$500 deal, your net profit would be only $180. But that would still be a return of 28 percent on the $640 you'd have invested, and you'd have $1,040 to reinvest. If you pyramid at the same down payment percentage, your holdings would multiply fast. But if you kept your payments down, you'd do just as well to hold on to it for a few years or until it starts rising faster, unless you see other land where you'd prefer to switch your money because of better prospects for rapid appreciation.

The Importance of Timing

If, however, there's reason to believe that the value will start rising faster soon, it would be a good time to go ahead and sell at only a 10 percent markup. Then you'd have twice as much land already leveraged when the acceleration begins, if you reinvested the $1,040 in $8,000 worth of land.

Land generally does not increase at a steady rate, but in fits and starts. In fact, you make the most money in land that's shooting up in value rapidly rather than steadily. If land actually did increase in value at a steady rate of, say, 33.3 percent every year, this would have a compounding effect. The 33.3 percent increase after the first year becomes part of what is increased by 33.3 percent the second year, and so on. The values would look like this:

Beginning	$ 4,000
After: 1 year	5,333
2 years	7,111
3 years	9,481
4 years	12,642

But it hardly ever happens exactly that way. If the value goes from $4,000 to $12,642 in four years, that would mean an *average* annual increase of 33.3, but the reality might be that it happened one of these (or other) ways:

Beginning	$ 4,000	$ 4,000	$ 4,000
After: 1 year	4,000	5,000	6,000
2 years	4,000	5,500	8,000
3 years	10,000	8,000	11,000
4 years	12,642	12,642	12,642

Pyramiding would not achieve anything in the first case until the end of the third year. In the second case, the best course would be to sell and reinvest after the first year and again after the third year. In the third case, doing so each year would be highly profitable.

The compounding effects of pyramiding are consistent and reliable. They're based on immutable mathematics. The best way to get the most out of pyramiding is to keep a close watch on your land's value increases so you can act at the most profitable time.

Though I don't know the details, a 35-year-old New York attorney turned $2,000 into several million dollars in a seven-year period recently by buying and selling real estate in a series of well-timed transactions that utilized the pyramid strategy.

Converting Interest Payments to Leveraged Investment

Interest costs are highest during the first year. The unpaid balance on which they are based keeps declining.This fact tends to favor not selling frequently, since the longer you pay on a land contract, the faster the balance owed goes down. This means also that the interest cost cuts less into your profit each year. But this is of little consequence compared to the benefits of credit buying leverage.

Your interest payments become converted to leveraged investment, anyway, during the pyramiding process. When you sell, the cash proceeds include the amount you had figured for interest costs. Unless you put it back in your checking account to replace what you had paid out in interest, you now have it for investment use. As a result, the money you pay for interest ends up helping you pyramid your profits, though it's not technically an investment when you actually pay it out.

Overnight Profits with Leverage

Leverage can maximize quick profits when you're able to buy land below the market value and sell it again quickly at the market price. If you can buy a $10,000 parcel for $9,000 because the owner is in a hurry to sell, then sell it for a quick $1,000 profit, you can double your money overnight when you only need to invest a $1,000 down payment.

If you did have $9,000 cash, you could keep $8,000 of it in case another such bargain came up.

Starting a Pyramid with No Money at All

You might even borrow $500 or $1,000 to swing such an overnight deal—or a slower one—and then pay it back out of the leveraged profits, keeping the rest to build your profit pyramid.

Another way to start with no money at all is to trade a car, a boat, a house or other personal or real property as your down payment. You can increase your leverage by trading expensive land for cheap land, such as a $10,000 suburban lot for 200 acres of $50-an-acre land—or a $2,000 vacation land lot for such acreage. One investor once traded the U.S. government 22 acres of California oceanfront for 14,145 acres of Nevada range land. Both tracts were priced at $142,000, but the Nevada land, at $10 an acre, had much greater potential for rapid, high leverage appreciation. A year after that trade, the Nevada land was up to $15 an acre.

Other Advantages to Credit Buying

When you buy land on credit, your investment is increasing in value even before you finish paying for it, often faster than you're paying for it. You can sell it for big profits before you complete more than a fraction of the payment.

During inflation, chances are good that it's rising in value faster than you're putting money into it, since each payment is worth less in comparison with the value of the dollar at the time you signed the land contract.

You complete the investment in cheaper, depreciated dollars than you originally agreed to pay. In effect, the price you paid is going down even while the value is going up.

Though your interest and property tax expenses are deductible against ordinary income on your federal income tax, your profits on investments you keep longer than six months are taxed at the long-term capital gains rate, which is half the ordinary rate. (You can deduct the interest and taxes from the profits, but you get only half as much deductability at the capital gains rate; deducting them against other income is legal.)

10

WAYS TO
MINIMIZE THE DRAWBACKS

No matter how good a technique is, no matter how effective an investment approach may be, there are bound to be some flaws and drawbacks. Nothing is perfect. Investing in well-located raw land has fewer drawbacks than any other type of investment, but still there are some problems. The best way to deal with this is to be aware of them from the beginning and be prepared to keep them to a minimum.

The most difficult aspects of investing in raw land are the waiting, and the costs you must pay while you are waiting.

If you pay cash, you put out your money and wait for the land's value to go up. Meanwhile, you pay the property taxes. If you buy with installment leverage, you also have additional payments to make and these include interest costs. Though you later recover some of the money through the deductability of taxes and interest on the federal income tax, that's only a portion of the amount you pay out and doesn't give you any immediate relief from the necessity of making the payments.

At the same time, there's usually no money coming in that you can use to offset the outgoing payments and expenses when you invest in raw land. After a year or two, it can get discouraging, especially if you're hit by financial problems. You may well begin to have doubts. You may even torture yourself with gloomy self-criticism and suffer intermittent despair. You wish you could use the money you're paying on a land contract or in property taxes to pay pressing bills. You are having an attack of nerves. One reason why some experts recommend against investing in raw land is the natural human tendency toward panic when money is going out and not coming in. The strain on your budget might pressure you to sell prematurely or at too low a price.

In addition, liquidity is low. There's no assurance that it will be easy to convert land into cash quickly when you need it without accepting a sales price below the market value. And it's usually difficult to borrow against raw land; most banks and other lending institutions will not lend money on raw land unless you're an established developer, a wealthy depositor or a friend of the bank's president.

How to Protect Yourself from the Dangers

There are ways to guard against these perils, however, and minimize the danger of their ruining your investments. One very necessary step is to avoid committing yourself for a bigger monthly payment, or other payment arrangement, than you can handle comfortably. Installment buying reduces the waiting problem, since you're not putting up the entire purchase price for the whole duration of the wait. But it requires current outgo, usually with no offsetting income. You should be sure not only that you can handle the payments and the taxes, but also that you can maintain a cushion in reserve for emergencies, too.

An important advantage in buying low-priced land in parcels that are not large is that it means low payments, low interest costs, and low tax bills.

Once you've started to make a profit and want to reinvest, you must still be careful not to overextend your resources. It's a good idea not to reinvest every last penny of profit each time, but to keep some of it in reserve—especially if you will have large payment obligations that you may have difficulty meeting. This is what I did with my $6,000 profit from the sale of 80 acres in northern Michigan. I reinvested $3,000, but kept the rest to insure my ability to make the payments. Later, when I could be sure of no problems, I could use it to buy more land.

This is another reason for spreading your money among several small or medium-size investments rather than staking it all on one big plunge. It's usually easier to sell off a small one if you need cash or must reduce your outgo. It's also not so bad to take a loss, if you have to, on a portion of your investment instead of the whole thing.

If you're buying on credit and things get so bad that foreclosure strikes, losing just one out of four or five parcels is less painful than losing one big property representing your total investment. An ability to make four-fifths of your payment obligations won't help you much if everything hinges on one big payment—but it can save four out of five smaller properties.

Deriving Income from Vacant Land

Sometimes you can find ways to get income from vacant land. In fact, this is a matter you should keep in mind when selecting an investment—whether there is any potential for income while you're waiting for appreciation.

Even vacant suburban land can sometimes be leased for farming, inflation gardens, or other temporary use. I rented my small plot of land north of Detroit to a farmer before the state took most of it. The income was only a few dollars a year, but every little bit is worth getting. Wooded vacation land might have salable timber, or wild blueberries that you can sell from a roadside stand. You may be able to rent space on vacation land for hunting camps or summer camping. Even if you don't take in enough to cover the interest and tax expenses, every penny helps.

There's also psychic income. When we had our 80 acres in northern Michigan we made frequent weekend trips to go picnicking and hiking in our very own woods, enjoying our land while its value was growing. It was a lot of fun, and that's worth something too.

The Use of Partial Sales to Prevent Trouble

You should be alert to problems in advance so that you're not caught by surprise. If you suspect ahead of time that you may have rough sledding, you can buy land in the first place that will be easy to split up for partial resale, or you can start making plans to sell one of your properties before the hard times actually arrive. That way you have a better chance of getting a profitable price.

Since the payments of $120 a month on my Michigan Upper Peninsula lake frontage sometimes verge on the burdensome, I've considered selling half of it. If I could get $75 a foot for 300 feet of the frontage in 1975, three years after I bought it, I would make a profit of about $9,800—a gross profit of $12,500 ($22,500 less half the $20,000 original cost) minus $2,700 in interest cost. That would be a return of 576 percent (192 percent per year) on a total investment of $1,700 in that 300 feet. After paying off my own land contract with $16,600 of the $22,500, I would have $5,900 cash for possible reinvestment, no further monthly payments to make, and the other 300 feet of frontage free and clear.

Or, I might be able to get the owner from whom I'm buying the land to let me pay off just half the contract, transfer title to the 300 feet I'm selling, and reduce my payments to $60 a month. Paying off half the contract with $8,400 from the $22,500 proceeds would leave me with $14,100 cash and monthly payments only half as large.

If you anticipate possible partial sales when you're buying on a land contract, it's smart to include in the contract a provision giving you the right to pay off portions and get deeds to those portions ahead of the complete payoff. The exact size and location of the portions can be specified, along with the amounts of partial payoffs, but it's not necessary. It's possible to have a provision whereby the seller agrees to convey title to whatever portion the buyer wishes to pay off at any time. Such a provision is sometimes called a release clause, though this term is more commonly used to refer to provisions in mortgages where portions of a property are released from the mortgage lien in return for partial repayment of the mortgage loan.

This device was used by a group of investors who bought 64.7 acres in a growing suburban area a few years ago. The seller kept a mortgage on the land, but agreed to release it in 11 different parcels upon payments of various amounts. When the investors found a buyer for a 7.6-acre parcel at $143,500 four years later, they got it released for $100,000, which they paid from the $143,500 sale proceeds, making a quick $43,500.

Using Credit to Resell Land You Don't Own

If it were not possible for me to find a buyer of 300 feet with $22,500 cash, I probably would find it easier to sell it on a land contract even though I haven't completed my own land contract purchase.

If I sell 300 feet for $80 a foot on a contract, with $4,000 of the $24,000 down and payments of $200 a month, I'd have the $4,000 in cash plus $80 more per month coming in than I'd be paying out. I could probably also get a higher interest rate than the seven percent I'm paying, and make a profit on the difference. (Too bad I'd have to pay ordinary income tax rates on that.)

I could also sell 100 feet, any other portion, or all 600 feet that way. If I sold 600 feet at $80 a foot for $48,000, with $8,000 down, I'd have $8,000 cash and a monthly income of $400 to pay only $120 on my contract.

Discounting—A Shortcut to Cash

Then, if I still needed cash, I could sell the land contract to a discounter who buys land contracts at a discount of 20 to 30 percent. This is also known as discounting a land contract. There are many real estate agents and well-to-do investors who invest this way because it affords a steady, very lucrative return on their money.

If I were to discount my $20,000 contract ($24,000 for 300 feet less $4,000 down) at 25 percent, I would get $15,000. With the $4,000 down, I'd have a total of $19,000 in cash—more than I would have netted in a cash sale at $60 a foot.

The discounter gets an eventual profit of $5,000, since he's got $20,000 coming for the $15,000 he paid, plus highly leveraged interest income. If the interest on the contract is eight percent per year, he's getting eight percent on $20,000 while having put up only $15,000. His interest income for the first month, for instance, would be $122.33. On his investment of $15,000, that's 9.4 percent. As long as he holds the contract, the effective rate of the interest he receives will be greater than eight percent.

To do this, you would have to get title to the 300 feet and transfer it to the discounter, have title to the 300 feet transferred directly to the discounter, or assign your land contract purchaser's interest in the 300 feet to the discounter (if he's willing to handle it that way).

Discounting is a safety valve that's available when you need to sell in a hurry to get cash or relief from financial pressure. You may still end up with less profit than you would have if you could wait for the right time to sell, but if you bought right in the first place the odds are that you will still do well. When I sold my 80 acres in northern Michigan, I used a form of discounting to get cash more quickly. I actually sold the land for $12,000 on a land contract rather than $11,000 in cash, with provision for a $1,000 discount if the buyer paid off the contract within one year, which he did.

Better a Wait Than a Loss

If things go so poorly that your land doesn't rise in value fast enough to cover the interest cost at first, you haven't much choice except to wait—or take a loss. If you can wait, the chances are that appreciation will catch up with interest cost, especially since the interest cost keeps decreasing as you make payments.

If you select your investment wisely in the first place, your chances of losing are remote. The worst that's likely to befall you is that you will have to wait longer than you figured. If unforeseen financial troubles force you to sell prematurely, or otherwise at a loss, that's not the land's fault. That can happen in any form of investment.

Stocks and mutual funds are more liquid than land; you can get your money in a few days. But if their value happens to be depressed when you need the cash, you lose. Land's lack of liquidity makes conversion to cash slower in a pinch, but basically it's no more disadvantageous than any other investment in that kind of crisis. And the other side of the liquidity coin, stability, is what makes land such a solid, low-risk route to big profits.

Other Safeguards in Credit Buying

As mentioned previously, be sure to get full title protection, preferably in the form of a title insurance commitment or policy, before you sign a land contract or other installment purchase contract. Some sellers may request that this be deferred until all the payments under the contract are completed and it's time to execute a title transfer through a deed. Don't agree to that. If there's any flaw in the title, or any impediment to clear title, the time to know about it is when you sign the original commitment, not after you've paid all the money. If no title insurance is involved, be sure to have a title search or abstract examination before you sign the contract.

If the seller is himself still buying on a land contract and does not yet have title, you should make sure that you are protected in case he defaults on his payments. For this, you should consult a lawyer. One way to give yourself some protection is to provide in the contract for return of all the money you pay if the seller is unable to convey title, but that won't avail you much if the seller goes bankrupt or disappears. An attorney can give you the best advice on the most effective protection in this regard.

Be sure to have your land contract or other installment purchase contract officially recorded. This can be crucial if a dispute or lawsuit should arise over ownership of the land with third parties. For instance, if the seller should sell the land again to someone else after selling it to you on a land contract, and the second buyer officially records his contract or deed before you record your contract, he would probably end up with the land. Your only recourse would be to attempt to get back whatever you had paid the seller. The same thing conceivably could happen in a cash purchase if you neglected to record the deed, but people don't seem to neglect the recording of deeds whereas many land contracts do not get recorded.

It's also wise to make sure that your installment purchase contract provides that you have possession of the land while you're buying it. Most land contracts do give possession to the buyer, but it's a good idea to double check, especially if you're to pay the property taxes.

Keeping the Property Taxes Down

Taxes are another expense you have while waiting for appreciation to make you wealthy. Sometimes you can arrange to pay taxes along with your regular payments on a land contract, but usually you must handle them separately. Taxes, however, are relatively low on undeveloped land, especially cheap land on the fringe of development. Low price means low taxes.

Since taxes are lowest of all in remote areas and places that have good potential for vacation or resort use but have not yet begun to develop, investing in such land is the best way to keep tax expenses low as well as the best avenue to low-price leverage.

Taxes can become an acute problem in suburban fringe land when values begin to rise under the impact of approaching development. If the land is reassessed for tax purposes after a sharp rise in nearby values, or if the local government reassesses every year, your tax bill might appreciate faster than your land—especially if the assessor compensates for infrequent reassessments by estimating what your land will be worth two or three years in the future rather than what it's worth at the time. On the other hand, you often can benefit from a lag of tax assessments behind true market value. It may be helpful, when selecting an investment, to find out the tax assessment frequency for the area.

Suburban growth also can bring costly special assessments for new water mains, sewer lines and road improvements. Though these can add strain to your pocketbook, the improvements usually increase the value of your land more than they cost. If taxes and assessments are rising, it means things are going the way you want them to. Development is arriving and prices are rising. If taxes prove burdensome, it may be time to sell, get your profit, and reinvest in something less burdensome.

Special Opportunities in Farm Land

The people who get hurt the most by rising taxes in growth areas are the farmers. Though the market value of their land is increasing because of development demand, it's not worth any more to them for farming purposes. The growing tax burden often forces them to sell to developers.

Authorities in some states have viewed this situation as undesirable because it helps drive up food prices and makes development harder to control. Some states are changing their tax laws to allow farm land to be taxed according to its use rather than its market value.

However, this has turned out not to help farmers as much as it helps investors and developers, who buy farm land, anyway, and then lease it back to the farmers for continued agricultural use. This keeps the taxes down until the land is sold or developed.

This is one way to invest in fringe land that produces income to offset tax costs and any interest costs—regardless of whether taxes are kept low by such special laws.

A small farm in the path of development often can be bought without much money, and mortgage financing is usually available from a bank or other lender. The advantage of a mortgage over a land contract is that, in the case of the mortgage, the buyer gets title at once, with the mortgage lender holding a lien. In practice, it doesn't make much difference as long as you get possession of the property when buying on a contract, and as long as you keep up the payments. But, if you default, it's easier for a land contract seller to foreclose than a mortgage lender. The contract seller is merely taking back what he already owns; the mortgage lender is taking what you own, and so he has to go through a more complicated legal process.

Protesting High Tax Assessments

Any time you believe your taxes are too high, don't hesitate to investigate and then avail yourself of the appeal process if you believe them to be unfair. Make sure you get notices of all proposed changes in assessment. Taxing authorities are usually required by law to give you such notice so that you have a chance to appeal an assessment before a tax review board. But sometimes the law requires only that such notice consist of publication in the local newspaper.

You can guard against a surprise tax increase by determining when assessments are made, how often reassessments are conducted, and when the board of review holds its public meetings. Then you can check on any possible increase in the assessed value of your land in time to protest it before the review board. If you miss the time for an appeal before the review board, you may be foreclosed from making a further appeal to a state tax commission.

When you make such a protest or appeal, you can take along whatever documents, records and statistics you need to argue your case. You also can take with you experts to help and assist you. You will have to decide for yourself whether the increase is great enough to be worth the time, effort and expense of contesting it. Fortunately, such situations do not arise often, especially if you stick to low-priced raw land. It's most likely to come up when your land gets rezoned from residential to commercial, a change that you otherwise welcome.

How to Benefit from the Preponderance of Advantages over Problems

Another advantage of raw, undeveloped land is that there usually are no maintenance expenses—nothing to keep in repair or good condition—unless you are so imprudent as to buy swampy land that has to be filled or lakeshore that's being eroded.

Compared to other kinds of investment, the drawbacks, problems, and pitfalls in land are few, and relatively easy to avoid or control. The main obstacle is the wait, and that's more an annoyance than a real problem. What's a little wait when you're sure of making big money?

One of the most crucial ingredients in successful land investing is patience. Never hurry, fret, or panic. Stay calm, cool, and alert to good buys and sharp timing. If you do everything reasonably right, it's just about impossible not to make handsome profits.

11

HOW AND WHEN TO SELL FOR TOP PROFITS

If you hit the mark when you buy fringe land for fast appreciation, you should not have to go looking for a buyer. As approaching development raises the land's value, it also attracts the interest of developers and
businessmen—and sometimes of speculators and other investors. If you have a
desirable location, they will be getting in touch with you. You won't have to go
searching for them.

In the case of vacation land especially, growth activity will attract other
investors as well as developers and users because it is early in the development
cycle.

Contacts from Real Estate Agents

In most cases, you will not hear directly from developers, businessmen,
industrial firms or other interested parties, but from real estate agents. Most such
buyers conduct their property searches through real estate brokers who maintain
regular contact with them.

Real estate agents are alert to opportunities for sales in areas where
development is attracting buyer attention even when they are not looking for land
to fill specific needs of buyers. Many will canvas an area from time to time to
find likely prospects for sale.

They go through property tax records to get the names and addresses of
owners and mail out form letters or postcards to solicit listings, promising top
prices from waiting buyers. Sometimes they offer a free appraisal, which gives
them a foot in the door if you respond.

Brokers sometimes do have buyers lined up for a specific parcel or number of parcels, but fear it would run up the price if that were known. Sending out a general listing solicitation to owners serves to camouflage their buyers' intentions until prices are set on most of the land by options or listing agreements.

How to Respond to Listing Solicitations

You can ignore such a solicitation in the mail if you're not ready to sell or if you wish to avoid appearing anxious to sell. Or you can make effective use of it to get up-to-date information on what your land is worth and how easy it would be to sell. Anytime you can get a good enough price, it might be smart to sell and reinvest again at low-price leverage.

You can respond to such approaches without seeming anxious to sell. It's also a good opportunity to begin making contacts with potential buyers without much effort on your part.

For instance, you can reply that you'd be interested in selling only if you can get a good price and ask the best price you might expect. If an agent in turn asks you what you want for it, don't give him a figure. Tell him it depends on what it's worth on the market and you're sure he is more qualified than you to say what that is.

A sample written reply might go like this: "Thank you for your inquiry about my property. I am not interested in selling at the present time unless I am able to secure a satisfactory price. Otherwise I prefer to wait for further appreciation. Any information you can send me as to the current value of my land and the price you estimate you could secure would, of course, help me to decide whether I would want to pursue the matter further at this time."

You have nothing to lose by this, and you might gain valuable information, not to mention a possible sale at a nice profit. If the price is high enough, it's worth paying an agent's commission.

What to Do If You're Not Contacted

If two or three years go by, however, and no one contacts you, not even a real estate firm on a routine solicitation of listings, there may be several possible explanations:

1. The real estate agents in the area are not aggressive.
2. Those who are looking for land there haven't noticed yours because you haven't put it up for sale.
3. You didn't hit the mark squarely when you bought and other land in the area is more desirable.

4. Development did not move as fast toward your land as you had anticipated.

5. Values failed to increase as rapidly as you had figured.

One or more of these factors might be involved. In any case, you are faced with a decision between taking action and waiting a while longer. As for action, you can move directly toward selling, learn more about why no one has contacted you, or do both in one step, by contacting a real estate agent about putting your land up for sale. This is the best way to get the latest information on your land's value and desirability.

The Advantages of Selling Through an Agent

It's usually wise to work through a real estate agent when you are selling land, more so than when you are buying. Though you must pay him a commission, his help often results in a higher price than you could get on your own—enough higher to more than offset the commission.

An agent ordinarily can put you in touch with buyers faster because they maintain contact with many. Those who specialize in commercial, industrial or investment property have particularly good access to a large number of interested and qualified buyers. It's not difficult for you to contact such potential buyers as developers, builders, oil companies, chain stores, franchise restaurants and other investors, once you learn the methods and the shortcuts. But a real estate agent almost always can do it faster and with greater ease.

The only way you can match a real estate agent's know-how, experience and contacts is to be in the real estate business for a while or to buy and sell real estate for several years. However, if you become that active and knowledgeable, you will appreciate even more the advisability of having an expert help you and take care of such details as paperwork and showing the land to prospective buyers.

When you're knowledgeable about real estate, you also know better how to select a competent agent, and how to utilize his services to your greatest benefit. Once you get started in a real estate investment program, in fact, you would do well to work through the same agent regularly. He will get to know exactly what you want and how you work. This will enable him to assist you effectively.

One extra service that a skillful real estate agent can offer is ingenuity in overcoming obstacles to bring about a sale where none seemed likely or possible. This can be a talent for getting two sides together in price negotiations, or a resourcefulness in helping buyers who are short of money find a way to swing a deal. A good agent will work hard at devising ways to get around snags, such as finding a place where a buyer can borrow funds or even accepting a promissory note for all or part of his commission.

The Exclusive Listing

When using an agent's services, there are different degrees of commitment you can make. There are three basic kinds of listing agreements. The one most frequently used, as well as the one preferred by agents, is the exclusive listing.

If you sign an exclusive listing, you give the agent the exclusive right to sell your real estate for a specified period of time—usually at least 90 days and sometimes six months or longer. This means that if you happen to find a buyer yourself and sell to him during that time period, you still will be obligated to pay the agent a commission.

An exclusive listing is also binding in another way. You are committed to sell at the price and terms detailed in the listing agreement. If someone makes a signed offer to buy at the price and terms specified, you can't change your mind. You're obligated legally to go through with the deal. If you do change your mind and refuse to go through with a sale, the buyer may be able to force you to do so through court action, and the agent may still be able to collect his commission whether or not the buyer forces a transaction. This is a good reason why it's important not to sign a listing at too low a price.

The main value of an exclusive listing to a seller is that the agent, since he has maximum protection, is more likely to make an aggressive effort to sell, including the expenditure of money for effective advertising.

Though they don't spread the information around freely, most agents will accept listings for shorter periods of time, sometimes even for only a few days. This happens when an agent has a buyer and declines to produce him unless he has the protection of an exclusive listing, while the seller doesn't want to enter a long-term commitment. A short-term listing is a workable compromise.

The Agency Listing

A slightly less restrictive agreement that some agents will accept is known as the agency listing, which is also called an exclusive agency listing. This gives the agent the exclusive right to act as your selling agent, but permits you to sell your land yourself without paying a commission. He may be unwilling, however, to give you a full sales effort, since he runs a greater risk of losing his time and money if you are free to look for a buyer, too. Agents generally are more willing to accept an agency listing if they already have good prospects on hand.

The Open Listing

A few agents will occasionally accept an open listing, which is actually just an agreement to pay a commission if they produce a buyer, but which gives them no exclusive rights. You can give an open listing to several agents at once. This listing can take the form of a letter agreeing to pay a commission, or even just an oral agreement. Again, agents most likely to accept such an arrangement are those who already have likely buyers on hand. No agent is going to spend much money on advertising or put much energy into finding a buyer in this circumstance.

Two of the agents who contacted me about my 80 acres in northern Michigan insisted on an exclusive listing before they would make any sales effort. But a third agent went ahead with only my agreement by telephone to pay him a commission if he produced a buyer at the price I wanted. He was the one who made the sale and collected a commission.

Variations in Commissions

The commission is sometimes subject to negotiation, though this is not widely known outside real estate circles. It happens more often in connection with vacant land and investment property than in the sale of residential property.

There usually is a prevailing percentage rate for real estate commissions, though it may differ from one city to another. Seven percent on residential property and ten percent on vacant and commercial property are common figures. But an agency may accept less than ten percent on vacant, commercial or other investment real estate if you press him on it, especially if the sale is large enough to make it worth his while.

If you sell through an agent, you must remember to take his commission into account when calculating the effects of leverage to determine the best time to sell. The commission must be deducted off the top of gross profit, of course. This can in some cases make a significant difference. If you can sell your land for a $5,000 profit, but must pay $3,000 in commission to an agent, it might be wise to wait a bit longer—say, until your profit is $10,000 and your commission only $3,500. A 10 percent commission will increase at the same pace as the sale price, but not as fast as the profit. For instance, here's how it would go if you paid $10,000 for your land:

Sale price	Gross profit	Comm.	Net profit
$12,000	$ 2,000	$1,200	$ 800
15,000	5,000	1,500	3,500
18,000	8,000	1,800	6,200
20,000	10,000	2,000	8,000

Deciding Whether to Sell on Your Own

If you don't want to pay a commission and believe that you can sell your land just as quickly for just as high a price yourself, it is possible to locate and contact potential buyers and follow through with effective sales methods on your own. You don't have to do quite as well or move quite as fast as an agent to come out ahead, since you avoid a commission. However, it does require more time and effort on your part, and you may have expenses for advertising, travel and preparation of documents. You will need to decide whether the commission you save exceeds what it costs to save it.

Much depends on how informed you are about real estate and your self confidence. Among the factors that can help you decide are:

1. How many potential buyers you already know about;
2. How many potential buyers you can reach easily;
3. How much information or advice you need to determine the most profitable potential use of the land and the highest price it can command on the market;
4. How difficult and costly it would be to locate and contact potential buyers.

You can get some information about potential use, buyer interest, and market value by talking to a real estate agent about listing your land even though you don't actually sign a listing agreement. However, it would not be realistic to expect him to be quite as informative before you sign a listing as he would be afterwards.

Advertising—The First Step Toward Selling on Your Own

One way to get more information to help you decide, and at the same time give yourself at least a small chance of saving the commission, is to make a stab at selling it yourself. If you don't get quick results, then you can decide whether to list with an agent or make a persistent attempt to sell your land without help.

The first step is to advertise, usually in the want ad section of a newspaper that circulates where you would expect it to reach a sizable number of potential buyers. If your land would be of special interest, or limited in interest, to a particular kind of buyer such as retail business firms, it's wise to concentrate your advertising in a newspaper's business section or in a special-interest magazine or newsletter for retailers in the area.

If you get replies from real estate agents, there's no need to run them off. Merely tell them you're not ready to sign a listing, but that you're willing to pay a commission if they make a sale for you that leaves you with the amount you want after their commission is deducted.

How to Identify and Contact Prospective Buyers

Another method of locating potential buyers is available if there is a particular use for which your land is suitable, such as a gasoline station or franchise restaurant. You can make direct contact with oil companies and restaurant chain executives.

You can get the addresses of such companies from the *Standard and Poor's Directory of American Corporations* at the public library. The directory lists each corporation's officers and often there is a vice president for real estate or development, or other appropriate official, to whom you can send a letter inquiring about any possible interest in your location. If no official is listed who seems the proper one, you can send it to the president or the executive vice president; it will surely be passed along to the executive who deals with real estate matters.

With regard to vacation land, there might not be many obvious prospects, but land development companies would certainly be among them. *Standard and Poor's* directory has an index of corporations according to their type of business.

While trying to drum up some interest in my landlocked .7 of an acre north of Detroit, I sent letters to 28 companies. Most of them were operators of fast food outlet chains or restaurant franchises, including Howard Johnson's and McDonald's hamburger restaurants. Some were national chains and a few were operating only in Michigan or the Detroit area. (I used the Detroit area *Yellow Pages* as well as *Standard and Poor's* directory.) Also included were a couple of motel chains.

Such a letter should give a description of the property and its location, along with an explanation of why it might be suitable for the addressee's business. Point out that you will be glad to send a map and further details, along with answers to any questions, if they have any interest. If you get a brush off, you at least have the name of someone to try again some time. If you don't get an answer, you might follow up with a phone call to inquire if the letter was received. It is not ordinarily an effective practice to phone without having first sent a letter.

Of the 28 letters I mailed, I received replies to 15. Of those, eight requested more information, which I sent. None of these resulted in a quick sale, but there was still a possibility of further follow-up in a couple of cases. In any event, I considered it a good response for my efforts, which cost me very little. I at least now have the names of several corporation executives who are interested in particular types of real estate.

Several of them sent me detailed specifications on the kinds of sites they need. You can get similar information by asking for it, even if you don't yet have any land for sale but just want the information to guide you in making your investments in the first place.

Mr. Steak Inc., for instance, informed me that it needs at least 30,000 square feet located on a major thoroughfare with a high volume traffic count near a good commercial and industrial area backed up by dense residential population of 75,000 in single family and multiple dwellings, preferably near a shopping center. Ponderosa Steak Houses need a minimum of 50,000 square feet with 150 feet of highway frontage. Denny's Inc. requires 40,000 square feet and frontage of 165 feet.

A Greater Need for an Attorney

Selling your land yourself increases your need for an attorney's services. A real estate agent handles such matters as drawing up a sales agreement and preparing a deed or land contract as part of his normal services, but you may have to arrange for that in some other way if you're not selling through an agent. Sometimes a buyer will have his attorney take care of these items if you ask, but it is often wise to protect your interests more carefully by having your attorney at least review the documents.

One thing to keep in mind is to be sure to get a significant deposit from a buyer—at least $500 and preferably $1,000—before you go to the trouble and expense of drawing up documents and ordering a title insurance policy. This is something else an agent would ordinarily handle as part of his routine. An agent also would do all the calculations involved in prorating property taxes to the date of sale and preparing a closing statement. If you have no agent, you must do that yourself. Also be sure you are paid by cashier's check, certified check or cash when you execute a deed.

Getting the Highest Price

However you go about selling, you will want to do whatever you can to get the best possible price—both by maximizing the intrinsic value and attractiveness of your land, and by using effective sales and bargaining techniques. These are among the steps you can take:

1. Make any improvements that will increase the value by more than they cost.

2. Eliminate or compensate for flaws and drawbacks at the lowest possible cost, such as getting trucks hauling dirt from construction sites to dump it free on any low spots. (If a buyer complains about such a flaw in negotiations, agree to have it corrected if you know you can do it inexpensively.)

3. Work among local authorities to get such public improvements as water lines, sewers and road paving that raise the value of your land. Many small communities in vacation and resort areas often are amenable to this in their eagerness to attract growth.

Rezoning for More Expensive Use

4. Get your land rezoned for more profitable use, or at least take steps toward rezoning on behalf of a serious buyer in those communities where a

rezoning application is considered only in connection with a specific proposed use. This involves learning about local zoning laws and politics. Talk to real estate agents and government officials to find out the identities of the real decision-makers, so you can ask them about procedures and chances. If you learn that a political contribution or clandestine payment would do it, don't go along. That's the time to proceed with the utmost caution and propriety. One possible course of action is to apply for the rezoning, anyway, while letting it be known you may challenge a rejection in court—though you should never say anything that can sound like a threat. If you have already established a reputation for fair and reliable dealings, you will always have a better chance for success.

Subdividing for Multiple Sales

5. Split your land up into smaller pieces that buyers can acquire more easily and which are better sized for immediate use. You can get more money per acre or square foot this way. Often you can do this easily and without expense if you divide your land up into just a few pieces, or if the pieces are still relatively large. But in some states you may become subject to costly regulations if you subdivide your land into many pieces below a certain size—into more than four pieces of 10 acres or less, for instance, in Michigan. Then you are getting into the kind of expense that extensive subdividing brings—such as for surveying and engineering, road construction, installation of utilities, platting, and government inspection fees. You may also run into zoning and health restrictions. Then you are becoming a developer in need of substantial additional investment instead of just an investor in land.

Packaging into Larger Parcels

6. Packaging your land with adjacent parcels when the best prospects for sale or use require a larger amount of land. This can be done by inviting owners of adjacent properties to join you in a sales effort, or sometimes by purchasing adjacent land, or by obtaining options to purchase.

Credit Selling for Fast Action

7. Selling on a land contract at a low down payment. More buyers are able to complete a purchase when you are willing to sell on credit, and you can usually get the highest possible price. You also can usually get enough cash in a down payment to continue your pyramid—though you must be careful not to accept so small a down payment that it will all go to an agent as his commission, since you ordinarily must pay the commission in cash.

Bargaining Techniques for Top Profits

It's always essential in bargaining never to be, or appear to be, anxious or desperate. If you are, at least have the good sense to conceal it thoroughly and try not to let it affect your judgment. Be friendly and businesslike, with courteous manners and a surface reasonableness. You should be able and ready to say, whenever things are not going well, that you're not all that eager to sell and mean it, or to get up and walk away regardless of how you feel underneath.

Your attitude should be that you'd like to complete a transaction, but only on satisfactory terms. You can be prepared to make some concessions, but only those you have decided in advance you can afford. Don't make concessions under pressure or in the heat of negotiations. If further concessions seem necessary, get away from negotiations at least briefly to study and evaluate the situation. Make concessions that cost you little but appear to cost you much. A real estate agent can be quite helpful in negotiations, not only by substituting his talents for yours but also by having a buffer effect at his disposal. He can, with impeccable logic, decline to make concessions without consulting again with you.

And, of course, the importance of setting at least a slightly too high price in the beginning is obvious. You can lower the price after the bargaining starts, but you can't raise it. So you want to be certain of not starting out too low.

Ingenuity at Surmounting Obstacles

You have a better chance of selling your land on your own if you have a knack for overcoming or circumventing obstacles to a sale. This can include finding ways to help a buyer get the funds he needs and eliminating drawbacks that make a buyer reluctant. One ingenious way to facilitate a transaction when a buyer has little cash is to get a bank loan on your own credit rating with the buyer to make the payments and get the land when the loan is repaid. This is similar to a land contract, except that you get more cash. Devising ways to surmount obstacles is a service, of course, that a good real estate agent may be well equipped by experience to offer.

No Need for High Pressure

You should stress your land's qualities and advantages, but high pressure is unnecessary and in the long-run ill-advised. You will generally do better, in dealing with people who buy the kind of land we're talking about, if you respect their intelligence and deal with them on a businesslike, factual basis.

It's all right to be unreasonable and to use effective psychology in getting people to respond in a positive way—such as appearing sincerely interested in their feelings and welfare—but don't be misleading or deceptive. You might make a sale or two that way, but on the average you'll lose more than you make, and in the process you'll get a reputation as a double dealer to be avoided. Besides, it's not a way of doing business that makes one feel good about himself.

The Value of Good Timing

Sharp timing is as important in selling as in buying. The best way to keep your timing well tuned is to keep informed on what's going on around your land and what's happening to prices. This can be done by maintaining contact with real estate agents, reading the newspapers, and probing the market occasionally by putting your land up for sale.

Ordinarily, the sooner you can sell at a good profit, the better. You can reinvest again at good leverage, and pyramiding almost always accelerates and multiplies the appreciation effect on your profits faster than waiting for a bigger profit from the original investment. The more your land rises in value, the more the effects of low-price leverage diminish. So it's important to keep alert to renewing your leverage power with turnover. When you're trying to decide whether to sell your $10,000 purchase for $18,000 or wait until it gets to $25,000, keep in mind that not-selling for $18,000 is equivalent to investing that $18,000 in that land at its current price. If its price is $450 an acre, it might be wise to reinvest the $18,000 in $100-an-acre land.

There are numerous variations, too—such as selling part of your holdings, or a portion of a parcel, not just to help you out of a cash crisis, but also to go at least partially into pyramiding while keeping some money in the original investment if prospects there are favorable for sharp price increases in the near future.

Prudence, patience and timing are the keys to profits in vacant land. Prudence and patience are easy enough to come by, and a good sense of timing will come sooner than you think once you get started.

After you start making big profits, you may be tempted to try other kinds of real estate, fancier deals and greater risks. It's by no means necessary to do so in order to get wealthy in real estate, but some people like variety for the challenge of it.

12

OPPORTUNITIES AND DRAWBACKS IN INCOME PROPERTY

It's hard to find a better investment than low-priced raw land on the brink of a sharp value rise. But there is at least one.

When you can find a piece of such land with the extra added attraction of regular income, you will have a property that pays for itself while it appreciates. In addition, the problems of monthly payments and taxes are eliminated and you may even get a small steady return while you wait for the big profits.

One Way to Get Self-Financing Land

A farm is one example. You can buy a small farm with a low down payment and rent it to someone who will raise crops or just live there. The rental income makes your payments, pays your expenses, and possibly produces a small profit besides.

Many people in recent years have caught on to this approach in states where farm land is rising in value under the impact of suburban growth. They know they can rent the farm or live there themselves, either farming the land on their own or commuting to work in the city while enjoying rural life.

Either way, the investment is small—just a down payment. If they rent, the rental income covers the payments until the land can be resold at a profit. If they live there themselves, the monthly payments are no more than they would pay for housing, anyway.

Many people profited this way accidentally during the suburban expansion of the past several years. To escape urban life, they moved out beyond the early suburbs to a farm. A few years later they were surprised to find that the city had caught up with them and they were suddenly wealthy because their land was in demand. I know of one man who bought a 40-acre farm on the corner of two main roads several years ago for $25,000 and recently sold it to a shopping center developer for $20,000 an acre.

A House on a Hot Spot

A faster way to make big money with this method is to buy a house, apartment, or other rental income structure on a piece of land soon to soar in value because of a coming usage change. An old house on a main road where commercial development is approaching is a good example of such an opportunity.

The idea is to buy the house with a low down payment on a land contract or mortgage and rent it. Your rental income makes your payments, pays your taxes, and covers your maintenance costs. If your timing is good, the price should still be low because the commercial use is still a bit in the future. Yet, it's not hard to rent for residential use. If you bring in enough rent to leave you a profit after you cover your outgo, all the better.

I came upon many such opportunities in the Detroit suburb of Troy several years ago—houses along main roads that I could have bought for $15,000 to $20,000, with $500 to $1,000 down, and which today sit on land worth up to $100,000 and more as commercial frontage. Unfortunately, however, I failed to take advantage of those opportunities.

My father did, however. He bought a house for $15,000 on a main road corner and moved in. Today the house is not worth a cent, since anyone who bought the land would tear it down. But the land is in the middle of a growing commercial area and is appraised at $80,000 to $90,000 even before any rezoning for commercial use. Once rezoned, it could be worth up to $200,000.

A main road near an area where a shopping center is likely to be built within the next few years is a good place to look for such an investment. It doesn't matter so much if the land takes longer to appreciate than you estimate. You've got money coming in every month, anyway. If you should fail to check out rezoning prospects carefully in advance or the situation changes to your disadvantage, you still have the income. Whatever small risk is involved in your selection of location is reduced further by the regular income.

Any improved real estate with rental income potential can be utilized in this fashion, including apartment buildings, small stores and shops, taverns, restaurants, office buildings and many others. But these usually require a larger initial investment. So, they offer less leverage as well as less accessibility to the small investor. Houses are the easiest because they require less money to get the real goal of your investment—the land beneath them.

More Income, More Problems

Though this approach rids you of cost problems while you wait, it also makes you vulnerable to headaches you don't get in raw land.

There's no guarantee that you actually will receive all the income you expect—or any of it, for that matter. Farm income is subject to a number of uncertainties, including one of the most unpredictable phenomena of all, the weather. Even if you are leasing the farm to someone else rather than raising crops yourself, a poor harvest may leave your tenant unable to pay his rent. In other types of income property as well, you may have trouble collecting the rent or getting tenants in the first place.

You also have more costs, which may leave you actually in worse shape than in raw land when income fails to materialize. Improved property, whether a modest residence, an apartment building, or a shopping center, costs more in property taxes and maintenance expenses. If things go less than perfectly—which, according to a basic law of nature, they usually do—you can find yourself paying out more money than you are taking in. Any income is better than none as long as the land goes up in value as expected, but if you can't rent at all or your extra costs exceed your income, you may be losing faster than the land is appreciating.

These drawbacks and risks, along with several others, are also important considerations in deciding whether to invest in income property for its own sake—for such other routes to real estate profits as rental income, buying and selling, and appreciation of improved property—rather than on the prospect of usage change for the land under the structures.

Pros and Cons of Dealing in Houses

Much money can be made in the buying and selling of residential properties, but it is a sophisticated game in which you need a quantity of operating capital, an immunity to bad luck, and a good deal of time to keep a constant watch for good buys. People who work in real estate are in a good position to trade profitably in houses because their work brings them into regular contact with good opportunities and they can use their commission to help buy them. When a real estate agent sells a house to himself, he can deduct his commission from the down payment. (This applies to any type of real estate, not just houses.)

Profitable trading in houses is a matter of buying them below the market value from sellers who are in a hurry to sell, then reselling quickly at the market value. A variation on this is to buy a house at a depressed price because it looks bad or needs repair, fix it up or decorate it, and resell at a profit. If you can't sell right away, you can rent, covering your mortgage payments and costs with rental income until you can sell.

Buying at market value in anticipation of appreciation is not feasible with houses. Residential real estate has increased in price considerably over recent years, and no doubt will continue to do so under the pressure of soaring construction costs. But increases in the prices of homes are relatively steady and slow, since no usage change is in sight that can produce a sharp rise in value. The limits of potential use are already determined by the existing structure. Even when using credit leverage, it's difficult to make much money from normal appreciation.

How to Make Leverage Work with Houses

But you can apply leverage effectively if you buy below market value. It may take a $20,000 home a year to increase in value to $21,000, and you'd have no profit at all if you pay a real estate commission. But if you can buy it for $17,000 because the owner is anxious or the house needs a coat of paint, then you can turn a quick profit without waiting for a year to pass. If you operate on a down payment of $500 to $1,000, your profit percentage can be substantial, even after paying a commission.

It's hard to get much low-price leverage, since prices already are high and the percentage of increase is low. But some is available if you deal in low-priced homes, where most buyers are to be found, anyway. For instance, if you buy a $50,000 home for $45,000 and resell at its true value, you make $5,000—a profit of 11 percent. But if you buy a $20,000 house for $17,000 and resell at market value, your $3,000 profit is a return of 17.6 percent.

The difference is sharper if you combine credit leverage with low-price leverage. If you made that $45,000 deal with $10,000 down, you would make 50 percent on your investment. But if you bought the $20,000 home with only $1,000 down, your profit rate is 200 percent.

Easy to Buy, Easy to Sell

Houses generally are easy to buy, due to the ready availability of mortgage financing most of the time—though not as easy as several years ago when homes could be bought with only $100 or $200 down, or no down payment at all, through the federal government's FHA or VA mortgage insurance programs. Those who qualify for the VA program under the GI Bill can still buy with no down payment, but only once. Otherwise, purchasing homes with only $500 to $1,000 down is usually possible only in low-priced properties, unless you have a banking connection that makes loans available to you at low down payments regardless of the purchase price.

One source of low-priced houses is the Federal Housing Administration, which repossesses homes on which buyers have defaulted on FHA-insured mortgages. But these homes are usually in bad condition and located in decaying neighborhoods. FHA has been stuck with thousands of such homes because of a fraud scheme perpetrated by unscrupulous speculators to exploit an FHA program developed in the late 1960's to give poor people a chance to buy homes.

The speculator would buy a rundown house in a slum area or deteriorating neighborhood for, say, $4,000, do a bit of cosmetic work on it for $500, get an FHA appraiser to approve a sale price of $10,000, and make a quick $5,500. He didn't care if the buyer later defaulted on the FHA mortgage, and neither did the mortgage company or the bank, since the mortgage was insured by the government. There have even been cases of fictitious buyers.

When default occurred, the mortgage holder collects its money from the FHA and the government gets the house. When the government sells the house at auction, usually for less than the amount of the inflated mortgage, the people who lose are the taxpayers. This unethical approach is not recommended, nor is buying such homes at auction. You might be able to fix them up and sell at a profit, but the risks are too great.

Since a house is the only kind of real estate that most Americans ever buy, it is the kind for which there are the most potential buyers. As a result, it's the easiest kind to sell, especially inexpensive homes, which not only comprise most of the mass market but also afford you some low-price leverage.

A house is also the easiest kind of real estate to sell on your own without the aid of an agent. The main steps in selling a home are advertising, holding "open house," making sure the house looks in top condition, and being able to help a buyer arrange financing. You can put an ad in the local newspaper as easily as a real estate agent, you have to spruce up your house yourself anyway, and residential mortgage financing is easy to arrange at a local bank, savings and loan association, or home mortgage company. About the only things you must do that an agent would ordinarily do for you is hold "open house" (usually on Sunday afternoons), show prospects around and answer their questions, and take care of some paperwork. Agents have readier access to buyers—especially if they belong to a multiple listing service in which many real estate firms pool their listings—but this is less an advantage in residential real estate than in other types because there are so many buyers.

Advantages and Risks of a Long-Term Approach

It's wise to keep in mind the profit potential when you buy a home as your own residence, even though profit should be a secondary consideration to having the kind of house you like in a convenient location. If you keep in mind the probabilities for future changes when selecting a location and are careful to get a good price, or pick a home that needs some improvements you can accomplish while you live there, you should be able to come out ahead if you ever have occasion to sell, just from normal appreciation.

Some investors in houses take a long-term approach, too. They buy houses and rent them out, letting the rental income build their equity. For a few, it's a retirement plan to have income producing properties already paid for when they quit working, or holdings they can sell if they want cash, or real estate to use as collateral for loans.

The extra risk you encounter in long-term investments, however, is a possible decline in value and an increased difficulty in renting due to a changing residential pattern and neighborhood deterioration. The longer you own a house, the greater the danger.

There are many other potential headaches, too, and most of them can affect short-term as well as long-term residential investments. These include poor tenants, difficulty of rent collection, higher fix-up or maintenance costs than expected, excessive demands on your time to look after your property (you can hire a real estate firm to manage it, but that won't be free), and a hard time reselling at a profitable price because of a tight mortgage money market, high interest rates, or other unforeseen conditions outside your control.

There's less assurance of an eventual value rise than in raw land, where such risks are practically nonexistent. You also need more time and have to make more deals to make the kind of money in houses that you can make more easily and faster in raw land.

Profits and Pitfalls in Apartments

It suddenly became popular a few years ago to invest in small multiple-unit rental properties like duplexes and four-unit apartments. There was a rash of books on how to make millions of dollars by buying, fixing up and selling apartments, starting small and building up to hundreds of units. Many of the books were written by people who told rags-to-riches stories about their own experiences. This coincided with a need for more housing and a change in federal income tax laws to permit greater deductions for depreciation. As a result, many new apartment structures of up to 12 units were built.

These were small enough for an investor to mow the lawn, replace broken windows, paint the walls, and handle other maintenance and fix-up chores, himself. Four-unit apartment buildings have been especially popular, since that's the largest that can be bought with no money down on a VA-insured mortgage. FHA-insured loans also facilitated investment in apartments with small down payments.

The enthusiasm began to cool, however, when investors started understanding from first-hand experience how burdensome the work and expense can be. They also discovered there is no guarantee against vacancies. In an apartment building with only four units, one vacancy means a painful drop in income of 25 percent. That is less disastrous than a 100 percent loss from inability to rent a house, or 50 percent from one vacancy in a duplex, but it's enough to put you in the red. Unexpected vacancies and unforeseen repairs don't hurt as much in big apartment complexes where they have smaller impact on income, and their average incidence is more predictable over a larger number of units, but you need a lot of money already in hand to start that big.

The Extra Profits in Depreciation Tax Shelters

The chief methods of profiting from investments in apartments are:

1. Regular rental income in excess of costs through efficient management;
2. Trading up to bigger buildings with more units, using profits from rental income and/or from selling and reinvesting;
3. Buying below market value and reselling, with rental income covering payments and expenses in the meantime (there are far fewer potential buyers than in houses, however, and it's practically impossible to sell without using an agent);
4. Buying a property in need of repair and improvement, fixing it up, and reselling;
5. Regular income plus appreciation profits.

Another method, which is somewhat similar to subdividing raw land except that it's rare, is to buy a building formerly used for other purposes—such as offices—and convert it into apartments. This sometimes can be done with a small investment if you can get construction financing or persuade contractors to work in return for a share of the profits.

In recent years, the federal government has introduced still another avenue to profit with its efforts to stimulate construction of multiple-unit housing, especially for the poor and the elderly. In addition to FHA mortgage insurance and rent subsidies, the government has provided tax shelter incentives through the deductability of accelerated depreciation costs against an investor's other income on his federal income tax.

A Few Tax Shelter Figures and How They Work

These benefits are attractive mostly to persons in high tax brackets, since they have the most to gain from deductions. In effect, a reduction in your income tax is the same as an after-tax profit. For persons in the top income tax bracket of 70 percent, profits can reach as high as 36 percent per year on their investment.

The small investor can't profit that much from a depreciation tax shelter, but he can use it to increase his return from a small apartment building.

The depreciation tax shelter works by creating a paper loss regardless of whether there is an actual loss, and regardless of whether there actually is any depreciation in the value of the property. In fact, the value of an apartment structure may actually increase while the owner is deducting the depreciation as a loss against other income.

As an example, let's say you buy an apartment building for $100,000. You calculate that $20,000 of this is for the land, $80,000 for the structure, and you will depreciate the $80,000 over 40 years—2½ percent per year ordinarily, but 3.125 percent per year on a declining balance under the accelerated rules. This would mean depreciation as follows:

1st year	$2,500
2nd year	2,422
3rd year	2,346

It would decline each year until 100 percent of the $80,000 has been depreciated. If you were to build a new apartment building or a complex of town houses, you could use 5 percent instead of 3.125, which is the figure for used apartment structures.

Any rental profits you receive after paying expenses and mortgage interest would be tax-free, in effect, up to the amount of the depreciation, since it is a deductible expense. If you're in the 50 percent income tax bracket and have $2,500 in profits, you would otherwise pay $1,250 in taxes. But with $2,500 in depreciation to offset the profits, you pay no taxes. You've saved (or made) $1,250 through the depreciation tax shelter.

If you have a profit before figuring depreciation of only $1,000, you have a $1,500 loss you can deduct against other income. At 50 percent, you save (or make) $750. Since you also saved $500 you didn't have to pay on the $1,000 profit, your total after-tax profit is again $1,250. If you broke even before depreciation, your $2,500 depreciation deduction against other income makes you, still, $1,250 on your income tax. The "loss" is actually a profit. If you're in the 70 percent tax bracket, the profit is bigger.

Enlarging the Tax Shelter with Leverage

If you invested $25,000 as a down payment, with the rental income making the mortgage payments, you would need only $2,500 pre-depreciation profit during the first year to make a return of 10 percent after taxes, since it would all be offset by depreciation.

That may not seem like a big advantage, but it gets bigger when you increase your leverage by purchasing with a low down payment such as on a 90-percent FHA mortgage, or a VA mortgage with as little as nothing down. The tax shelter also gets bigger as the amounts go up.

If you put only $10,000 down on that $100,000 deal, you can deduct depreciation on the full value of the building even though you've put up only 10 percent of the cost. An after-tax profit of $2,500 becomes a 25 percent return. If you broke even before depreciation, your income tax savings of $1,250 would be a respectable return of 12.5 percent. If you're in the 70 percent tax bracket, your profit would be $1,750, or 17.5 percent. On the other hand, if you're only in the 20 percent bracket, your profit of only $500 represents a mere 5 percent return.

If you qualify for a VA mortgage through military service, you can buy up to four units for up to $70,000 with no down payment at all. (One catch here is that you can use the GI benefit only once; another catch is that you're supposed to live in one of the units, yourself.) This means you can acquire ownership gradually with your rental income while making no investment whatsoever as long as the rental income covers your mortgage payments and expenses. You have infinite leverage. The depreciation writeoff possibilities increase the chances that you can make an annual profit besides. If you break even otherwise and deduct the depreciation from other income, you can make $250 a year even in a 20 percent tax bracket. On no investment, that's not bad.

The benefits expand substantially when you deal in high-priced properties. On a new $1,000,000 apartment building, the accelerated depreciation would be, say, $40,000 the first year. If the project breaks even except for depreciation, you'd have a $40,000 "loss." In a 70 percent tax bracket, this would be a savings, or after-tax profit, of $28,000. If it cost you $100,000 to make the investment on a 90-percent mortgage, you'd be making 28 percent on your money. And if the property made a cash profit, it would be tax-free up to $40,000. If your depreciation losses were only $20,000 a year, and you were in the 50 percent tax bracket, you'd have your $100,000 back in after-tax profits in less than four years. But, as you can see, it takes big money to do this by yourself.

A Couple of Catches, However

If things go so badly that you have an actual cash loss in addition to depreciation, you can also deduct that against other income—to the extent that it exceeds the increase in equity ownership you gain through the mortgage payments. You may even be required to invest additional funds to avoid default, however, and that is a risk you face in the event rental income falls short or costs run too high.

Another catch is that you will have to pay income taxes on all those indirect profits through depreciation when you sell. This is because you must reduce your cost basis for calculating profit by the amount of the depreciation. If you've depreciated $40,000 of a $50,000 building and then sell it for $60,000, you must pay taxes on $50,000—the difference between the adjusted cost basis of $10,000 (original cost of $50,000 minus $40,000 depreciation), and the selling price of $60,000. However, you still come out ahead. You pay these taxes at the capital gains rate, which is half the ordinary rate (or less than half if your bracket is over 50 percent). Your benefits from the depreciation were derived at the ordinary rate. (The capital gains rate doesn't apply if you don't hold the property six months or longer, but then depreciation is insignificant.)

You even must pay capital gains taxes on depreciation if you lose the property through foreclosure. You're obligated for taxes on the difference between the adjusted cost basis and the amount of the mortgage, if the mortgage balance is greater. For tax purposes, a foreclosure is treated as a sale for the amount owed on the mortgage.

Still another risk is that the U.S. Congress can at any time change the tax laws to make apartments a less attractive investment—and therefore harder to sell, as well.

A Few Words of Caution

All this tricky maneuvering with tax benefits is best to be avoided if you're not in a high tax bracket, or if you don't have much cash and are not approaching it as a group venture with other investors. A small investor can benefit slightly from depreciation writeoffs in apartment unit investments—enough to turn a marginally bad investment into a marginally good one—but he can't really make big money fast that way and the risks are high.

Nevertheless, if you like that type of investment, anyway, the tax shelter device can help you build large holdings in apartments over a period of years through trading, selling and reinvesting in more units, or investing rental income profits in additional structures.

It's a good idea for the small investor, however, only if he can start with little money—a low down payment or none at all, on an FHA or VA mortgage, on a land contract, or through a banking connection that enables him to borrow the full purchase price when it's 20 to 25 percent below market value. Ordinarily, if you have enough cash to make a $10,000 down payment, you can do better faster in raw land. But if you can get in for little enough money and get good leverage, apartments can be worth trying. You can even use it as a way to start from no cash at all and get some, through rental profits, to invest in raw land.

Losing Money on No Investment at All

The biggest flaw in all this is the risk of losing a lot of money if things don't go right. Even when you buy an apartment building with no cash at all, you can end up losing money if your cash flow is too low to cover your costs, or your property declines in value because of a poor location. If things don't go right in raw land, you at least don't lose any additional money and have a good chance of doing all right in the end after a longer wait. But in apartments (and other rental property), you can keep losing more each month.

The risk is smaller with a new apartment structure or one that's less than ten years old and is located in a growing or relatively new area. You still lack flexibility in that further use change is unlikely that would produce a sharp value rise (though it does happen occasionally because of a change in a shopping center location or a new freeway). But at least you can be relatively sure that the property will increase steadily in value (unless the new freeway ends up right next to it) and you will be able to attract good tenants. This is especially true during a time of housing shortages brought on by a construction slump such as in recent years. Maintenance costs also are lower in newer properties.

But a less desirable location in an older neighborhood, even one that now appears stable, can be affected adversely by a deterioration in the area's character. One reverse effect of suburban growth on property values is to decrease the values of property in older sections of the city. Once a neighborhood starts to decay, it is hard to stop the snowball effect. Residents concerned about property values rush to get out, which pushes values down further. Sometimes unscrupulous real estate agents start "blockbusting"—encouraging more owners to sell, and accelerating the deterioration process.

If your apartment building gets caught in a trap like that, it won't do you much good to have bought at a bargain price. Your tenants start moving out, their replacements pay less and cause more problems, your costs increase while income falls, and you will have a hard time getting a good price if you want out.

The Difficulties of Controlling Costs

The cost of operating even a small apartment building can easily get out of hand, especially in a time of inflation. There are plumbing repairs, heating problems, water tank malfunctions, water leaks in the basement, electrical failures, landscaping maintenance, property taxes, insurance, interior and exterior painting, defects and problems you failed to spot before you bought, and troubles no one ever thought of before. A real estate management firm to take care of these things will charge a fee, usually ten percent of the rent, and you still will have to pay many of the other costs, too.

It's been estimated that taking care of a small apartment house can use up 500 hours a year if you do the maintenance yourself. In a larger one, it's unavoidable to hire out most of the work done.

It's crucial to get an accurate figure on total costs before you buy, so that you can make an accurate estimate of net income. If the spread between the mortgage payment and the rental income barely covers expected costs, it's too close for comfort. If unforeseen expenses occur or you have trouble keeping the units occupied, you may well need some red ink.

The Uncertainties of Income

Even when costs are well-controlled, certainty of income depends on maintaining a certain level of occupancy. But there's no guarantee you won't have more vacancies, and longer vacancies, than you counted on. In calculating potential income, you usually deduct a percentage of the rent, customarily three to five percent, to allow for losses due to vacancy. But, if your vacancy rate exceeds that, your calculations aren't worth much. And the fact that there hasn't been a vacancy in 10 years is no guarantee that there won't be three tomorrow.

When something does go wrong, it tends to feed on itself and grow like a cancer. If vacancies or costs go up or the neighborhood starts fading, it's harder to keep the apartments in good shape to attract good tenants. If you accept lower rents and poorer tenants, you've got more problems. You're caught in a vicious downward circle.

Before you know it, you're inundated with problems. You can't afford to keep the structure in compliance with the housing code. Tenants have formed a union and are withholding their rent until you do comply under one of the new landlord-tenant laws that subject you to more restrictions and obligations than used to be the case (and make it harder to evict undesirable tenants). And you can't sell the property except to a slumlord who will pay only a highway-robbery price. The result is the same as if you had deliberately set out to bleed the property while letting it deteriorate.

Opportunities in Slum Properties—Unsavory and Otherwise

The only sensible alternative to selling at a loss to a slumlord is to become a slumlord yourself. Learn how to avoid fix-up costs by frustrating enforcement of the housing code through ownership juggling among dummy corporations. Hire a lawyer who knows how to stall legal action indefinitely. And bribe the housing inspectors.

Now you want poor tenants who turn over their welfare checks to you and don't care if you never fix up the place. Income may not be high, but costs are almost nil. In slum properties, the profitable method is the opposite of ordinary good property management. If you don't mind the danger of ending up this way, the risks may not bother you. But it wouldn't be anything to be proud of.

Investing in slum areas, whether residential, commercial or vacant, on the prospect of sharp appreciation during eventual redevelopment can be similar to buying raw land on the fringe of new development. But there's a big difference in the time element.

There are sure to be enormous profits in buying up inner city land at depressed prices, but it's impossible to predict accurately how long it will take for urban redevelopment to revitalize such areas—even harder than projecting how quickly suburban development will overtake a fringe area. Much information can be obtained from local planning authorities on a city's redevelopment plans, but such plans have a way of falling through or bogging down far more often than they reach fruition. So the usefulness of such information is questionable.

The Risky New Fad in Condominiums

There's been a flurry of investment interest recently in a new kind of apartment structure called the *condominium*. But several problems have already surfaced that threaten to diminish its appeal.

A condominium is an apartment that you buy rather than rent, somewhat like buying a house except that all you get is an apartment unit plus a fractional interest in the land underneath the structure and the shared parts of the structure, such as the swimming pool, recreation room and laundry room.

Most people who have bought condominiums so far did so when they were new, usually in a project similar to a new residential subdivision or a retirement-vacation land development project. Some have been plagued by the same kinds of woes that crop up in development projects, such as swimming pools that never get built and developer bankruptcies that leave buyers with no title and no refund.

Snags and problems also have begun to show up when condominium owners decide to sell. It's been found that common ownership of the land and some parts of the structure introduce complications and confusions into legal aspects of ownership, raising a specter of uncertainties about clear title. If this problem cannot be solved, the difficulty of reselling condominiums may discourage original sales.

Condominiums tend to be high-priced, anyway. Making a profit by trading in them is no easier—and perhaps harder—than dealing in single family houses. It's not a good investment for the average investor except as a way to develop and sell vacant land he already owns, which also can be done with regular apartments.

Opportunities in Commercial and Industrial Income Property

Building on your land and selling or leasing is also a method of realizing profits in commercial and industrial land. You can ordinarily get mortgage financing to pay for construction of apartments, condominiums, stores, offices, and small industrial shops if you own the land free and clear. But it might not be so easy to get if you are still paying on a land contract. One way to make it easier is to get signed lease commitments from prospective tenants. But then, of course, you have become a developer instead of just an investor. You might even try a shopping center.

If you buy raw land in anticipation of potential commercial, industrial or multiple-dwelling development, be sure to investigate ahead of time the prospects for getting any necessary rezoning. It's more important here than if you plan merely to resell the raw land. If land is not already zoned for the use you plan to develop, you first have to secure the proper zoning.

Profitable investments can also be made in existing office buildings, stores and industrial shops of all sizes. As in houses and apartments, you get depreciation deductions (though not accelerated), you can buy and resell or invest for rental income, and you may do well in reselling (but only if you buy below the market value). Some developers carve up big old buildings into small shops for leasing or for sale as industrial condominiums. Business and industrial firms sometimes sell their buildings to investors in a leaseback arrangement because renting gives them more tax advantages than owning. This gives the investor a guaranteed rental income, but his protection against rising costs depends on the details of the agreement.

This is a highly specialized type of investment, and few opportunities are open to the small investor with little cash. Even a small store or office building can require a sizeable down payment—unless you can buy well below market value and have a banking connection.

You might want to get into this after you've made several thousands in raw land, but the profit opportunities aren't any better, actually, than in raw land—unless the rental income is subject to little risk of interruption or the property is sure to keep rising in value (such as a new suburban shopping center or a good location near one).

In any case, the risks of higher costs and income drops can never be avoided with certainty. The prospects for profitable use change are remote. And the location can become undesirable—for such reasons as a change in transportation patterns brought by a new freeway, or competition from a new shopping center a mile away.

Raw Land Still the Best Bet

When comparing risks and certainties, raw land always comes out as a better investment than improved property, especially for the small investor, unless it's the land beneath the structure you're after. Improved property means regular income, and raw land brings a sometimes tough wait. But improved property entails greater risks and more work, while raw land produces bigger profits faster, takes less time, and can be more fun.

13

HOW TO GET THE MOST OUT OF GROUP INVESTING

A group of people who pool their resources can accomplish more than the individuals on their own.

When you join with others in a real estate investment, your contribution to the investment has a share in the greater power created by the grouping. In a sense, it's a form of leverage.

A Way to Get in on Bigger Deals Faster

Group investing enables you to participate in investments that you have too little money to handle, or would prefer not to attempt, by yourself. A group can buy large tracts of low-priced vacant land that none of its members could buy on his own. It can buy apartments and office buildings more easily. It is better able to subdivide raw land or develop a shopping center, condominiums, or an industrial park.

Group investing also spreads the risks and the costs. If the group's apartment building loses money, only part of the loss affects you. A group can cope better with unexpected costs in development and in the maintenance of income property. It can more easily gather the resources to hire outside services from consultants, management firms, attorneys and other experts.

When there's work to be done, such as scouting for investments, checking records and maps, or painting apartment interiors, group members can share that, too. A group can include such experts as an attorney or an accountant who can make part of his contribution to the group effort in the form of legal services or tax expertise. In some groups, you can be a silent partner who does no work at all.

The three men who bought up land south of Dayton, O., where the multi-million dollar Dayton Mall now stands, knew that none of them could do it alone. But, together, they made a fortune.

The Other Side of the Group Coin

On the other hand, you get only a portion of the profits, the depreciation writeoffs, and the control. Often you have little or no say in the decisions, depending on the type of group. Your money may be invested, used, managed and manipulated without your knowing whether it's being done in accordance with your preferences or not. Your money might be unwisely invested, mismanaged or even stolen, while you're helpless to prevent it.

The price you pay for the extra power in grouping is the danger of losing access to your share of the power. Your share of the profits may end up depending on the whims of others if you can't influence the investment decisions or the distribution of profits.

The amount of control you can exercise in a group investment depends on the type of group and your ability to assert yourself.

Simple and Complicated Partnerships

The oldest and still the most common form of group investing is the partnership, but there are many kinds of partnerships and countless variations in relationships among partners. In its simplest form, there are two or more members who agree, usually in writing, to equal divisions of the investment, the work, the obligations, the control, and the profits.

In a partnership of two, you ordinarily retain at least 50 percent of the control, though it can be more or less. In partnerships of more than two, ordinarily each person is in a minority and cannot directly control the group's activity without the support and agreement of other partners. To influence a group in a direction he desires, an individual must be a strong and persuasive personality, or be adept at forming alliances. It's often necessary in a large group to designate one or two persons formally or informally to take charge and make decisions, subject to approval of the group, in order to avoid floundering for lack of decisive leadership.

Partnerships are common among business ventures, but can be used just as effectively for investing. If you come upon a parcel of land that's a superb investment but it takes $5,000 to make the deal and you have only $2,000, one solution is to find a partner or two interested in putting up the rest.

Equal-share partnerships, of course, can be made complicated by exceptions and special agreements. Partnerships automatically get complicated when the partners are not equal. Sometimes one partner will contribute the money, another the work. Or there will be different investments by each partner and different sharing arrangements for the obligations and profits.

This is usually the case in partnerships formed for tax shelter investments in new apartments, shopping centers and other large projects that need a lot of capital. In a $1,000,000 apartment venture requiring $100,000 in "front money" to make a down payment on a 90-percent FHA mortgage, a partnership could be formed of 10 investors who each put in $10,000. But in practice, there are different numbers of investors who put in varying amounts of "front money" and share in the depreciation writeoffs and other profits proportionately.

Advantages and Drawbacks of the Limited Partnership

One special form of partnership that's often used in apartment projects and other big ventures is the limited partnership. Here there is a general partner, sometimes the developer or the construction firm, that assumes responsibility for building or operating the property. In addition there are several limited partners who put in equal or varying amounts of cash, but do not play an active role in development and have limited liability if the project should fail, somewhat like a stockholder in a corporation.

A small investor may find such partnerships appealing as a way to invest in big real estate that he could never handle by himself. Yet, as a limited partner, his investment would be at the mercy of the competence and integrity of others. The risks may well not be worth the potential profit, especially if the investor is not in a high enough tax bracket to derive large benefits from the tax shelter. Most investors in such ventures are doctors, lawyers, businessmen, entertainers, sports stars, and others with large incomes and a desire to invest in ways that do not require their frequent attention. They do not always turn out well.

Many a limited partnership has lost money, for instance, in a government program to upgrade housing in inner city areas by rehabilitating the interiors of old, rundown apartment buildings that have basically sound structures. This FHA program induced developers and builders to rebuild the interiors of substandard buildings for renting to low- and moderate-income families by offering special incentives in addition to the ready availability of FHA mortgage insurance. These included superaccelerated depreciation writeoffs, subsidies on mortgage interest and rent, and extra profit gimmicks. The depreciation could be written off entirely over five years at 20 percent per year, telescoping the writeoffs into the early years far more intensely than in new construction.

But thousands of these projects across the nation have failed and gone into default, even before much profit from the depreciation tax shelter could be realized, because of loopholes and loose enforcement of regulations. So much money was siphoned off the top, legally and otherwise, by consultants, money "finders," speculators, "packagers" who lined up properties for investors and developers, inflated construction costs, real estate commissions, and mortgage company fees, that too little money was left to make the projects work. The result has been a mixed bag—on one hand a lot of badly needed housing for poor people and the elderly, but on the other hand a national scandal of millions of dollars in projects repossessed by the federal government because they can't pay their way.

Similar things can go wrong with any limited partnership project. The only way you can control the situation is to organize the project yourself, and be the general partner—or have some special arrangement that gives you control. But, to do that, you must either have big money already, or be in the local real estate and development establishment. No one is going to put his money into your hands for such a venture unless you are known for success in such endeavors or command the respect of prominent persons. It is no game for the small, independent investor unless he has a few thousand dollars he can afford to risk in someone else's care.

Improving the Odds by Including the Influential

One function that a group approach can serve is to gain the acceptance and help of prominent and influential citizens by bringing them into the group. I know of one investment organization that includes judges, a sheriff and several other local officials as well as leading businessmen. Whether or not the group gets any improper assistance from the officials' associates on local zoning boards and other governmental bodies, the presence of such dignitaries in the group certainly doesn't hurt it. There is usually at least one such group, and often several, in every community.

Sometimes local officials are exposed as having secret interests in groups or companies that benefit from their votes or other influence on rezoning requests or master land use plans. The officials' main mistake in such cases is keeping their connections secret. If they openly state their interest and abstain from voting, they'd still get the benefit of their friendships and alliance among their colleagues without compromising their honesty.

The High-Powered Approach Called Syndication

Not all partnerships are strictly local. Some that take on huge projects like office towers, shopping centers and vacation land developments attract investors from across the nation and from all kinds of sources. Some individuals make a full-time business of putting together such investment projects and "selling" shares in them. Such groups are often called *syndicates* rather than partnerships, and the organizing of them is called *syndication*.

Syndicates usually are a form of limited partnership, except that most of them are tightly controlled by the organizers and managed by real estate professionals. They almost never are as loosely gathered as a small group of investors in one locality who entertain an urge to take a crack at a few town houses.

Syndicates generally include high-powered types who are accustomed to moving in big-money circles. This is not a milieu that the small investor finds accessible or comfortable. It takes sizable investments and a willingness either to let others decide the fate of your money, or to jump in and assert yourself, which isn't easy if you're new to the scene.

Real estate syndication was started in the late 1940's as a means to raise the big chunks of capital needed to finance major construction. A New York real estate and tax lawyer named Lawrence A. Wien has claimed credit for thinking up the technique. Wien has been quoted in *Forbes* magazine as saying:

> What I wanted to create was a vehicle that could achieve the yield objective of, say, 12 percent and at the same time avoid the corporate income tax. I analyzed the tax statutes, and realized that if I could create a partnership that was not engaged in business but was merely receiving a fixed return on capital investment through a conduit, then the investor would only have to pay an individual income tax. In addition, I could save half or more of his return from any taxation because part would be a return of capital.

The Internal Revenue Service finally went along with this, and syndication has been popular among wealthy investors for more than 20 years as a system that permits real estate to be bought, sold and operated for profit in little pieces by several investors.

Most syndicates do not view themselves as devices for investment by the average citizen, but as elite groupings of astute, already-successful investors. However, some syndications of various sizes and specialties have in recent years begun to sell "units" to the public from $2,000 and up, offering returns of 15 percent per year or more from tax-sheltered apartment houses.

Investing in Corporate Fashion

Forming an investment corporation is also a common method of group investing. It's an approach usually found among experienced investors who find the corporate structure and its limits on shareholder liability more useful, for tax purposes and other reasons, than direct writeoffs against personal income for depreciation.

It also tends to be a form favored by small groups rather than a method of involving the public in real estate investment. In many states, in fact, such corporations are careful to keep their number of stockholders below a certain figure (like 15 or 25—the number varies from state to state) to avoid becoming a corporation subject to "blue sky" laws that regulate the sale of securities to the public.

Large corporations in the real estate field tend to be developers, rather than investors, that profit from buying and selling or just collecting rent, though some large corporations do buy up large tracts of land for appreciation or future development. The shareholders of such firms are investing mostly in a business operation and only incidentally in real estate.

A corporation can invest in all types of real estate, just as an individual. The owners can profit just as much, depending on their tax situation, and have the advantage of the corporate protection against unlimited losses.

Though it's easy for small investors to get into real estate through purchase of stock in big real estate investment and development corporations, or shares in a mutual fund that includes real estate investments, this is not much different from investing in any other kind of stock. The stock might produce a good dividend and a rise in value, but then again it might not. The fact that real estate is basically a good investment is no guarantee that you won't invest in a bad company.

Congenial Group Investing Through an Informal Club

One of the most popular forms of group investing for small investors in recent years has been the investment club. This is a group of individuals that often is organized among relatives and friends who meet at a different member's home each month, agree to $10 a month dues for the investment treasury, include a real estate agent among themselves, invite various experts to speak at their meetings, vote on what real estate to buy and sell, and have a social hour with beer and pretzels after each meeting.

Many investment clubs adopt formal charters and by-laws, elect officers and appoint committees to perform various tasks. In most areas such formalization is necessary for legal purposes, but the clubs function informally in practice. Often the number of members is limited and rules are set up for a member to get his money out, including his profits, if he leaves the club.

If you'd like to start or join an investment club, there may be an association of real estate investment clubs in your state that would be glad to give you assistance and information. A real estate agent should be able to tell you how to find out about any such association in your area. No doubt he'd also be willing to help you start a club, too, since it might mean sales for him.

The New Fad—Real Estate Investment Trusts

In recent years, there's been a resurgence in the popularity of a device first introduced in the 1850's to give small investors a more direct slice of big real estate projects than ownership of corporation stock. It's known as the *real estate investment trust*, or *REIT*.

The REIT lies somewhere between a real estate syndication or partnership and a typical business corporation. It is similar to a mutual fund. A REIT sells pieces of real estate investment in the same fashion as a syndication or partnership and gets similar tax breaks, but the pieces are much smaller. They're more like shares of stock or mutual fund shares, they're sold to the public in much the same way, and their sale is regulated in similar fashion. A REIT is required to issue a prospectus giving full disclosure of all facts, and to register with the appropriate government agency before it can sell shares to the public.

While offering the same no-fuss, no-work, just your money deal as investing in the stock market, the REIT is also just as risky as stock or mutual fund shares. You're investing in the wisdom and honesty of the trust's management as well as its portfolio of holdings. Despite the tax break the REIT gets under federal income tax laws, the return is much the same as you'd get from an investment in the stock market—from 6 to 9 percent in normal times. Furthermore, shares in a REIT are attractive mainly for income and long-term growth; you're not likely to make a quick killing even though you're subject to risk of a quick loss.

Three Kinds of REITs

There are many sizes of REITs and various specializations. But there are only three basic types:

1. *Equity Trusts*. These invest in ownership of real property, including residential, commercial, industrial and vacant land. The primary source of revenue is rental income.

2. *Mortgage Trusts*. These engage in the lending of money and derive revenue from interest on construction loans, mortgages and other liens, both short-term and long-term, and from discounts and commissions on mortgages bought and sold.

3. *Combination Trusts*. These invest in both ownership and in mortgage financing.

Few if any trusts attempt to derive a major portion of revenue from the appreciation of raw land—at least not the larger ones—though some small private trusts do speculate and invest in vacant land.

A REIT is an unincorporated association that may own partnership interests as well as real property and mortgages. It operates as a business trust. The REIT lost its appeal for several years after it was made subject to the corporate income tax in 1935, but enjoyed a revival after 1960 when Congress gave it the same tax-exempt status that mutual funds and other regulated investment companies enjoy.

Trusts and associations in this category are exempt from corporation income taxes on earnings distributed to shareholders if 90 percent or more of the earnings are distributed. The shareholders pay the tax, but escape the double taxation to which corporation stockholders are subject. In addition, some of the earnings are taxable as capital gains instead of ordinary income, and some of the income is not taxable at all because it's distributed as a return of capital (such as income attributable to depreciation).

A Brief Look at One Small REIT

The prospectus for a recent issue of 500,000 shares at $10 in an Ohio REIT, *Investors REIT One,* told prospective investors:

> The purpose of the Trust is to provide investors an opportunity to participate in the advantages of real estate investment normally available only to those with large resources. These advantages include:
>
> 1. The opportunity to receive tax-sheltered income.
> 2. The means of investing in substantial real estate (which the investors could not undertake individually);
> 3. The opportunity to obtain the protection against inflation that real estate historically has offered when currencies have been subjected to inflationary pressures; and,
> 4. The opportunity to secure the benefits of expert investment counsel.

This trust has investments in motels, mobile home communities, apartments, car washes, vacant property and real estate loans.

Now, the Bad News about REITs

Despite the flexibility in spreading the investment over a variety of real estate, much like a mutual fund reduces risk by spreading it among numerous holdings, plus the basic stability of real estate and good leverage in their investments, real estate investment trusts are as unstable as common stock.

The value of REIT shares can go down even while land values go up. After enjoying a popularity boom in the late 1960's and early 1970's that led to the establishment of some 200 REITs, they fell on hard times with the rest of the economy in 1974–75. This left the REIT exposed as much less desirable than direct investment in real estate.

When you buy shares in a REIT, you delegate the management and maintenance burdens to experts so you can prosper at your leisure, except there's no guarantee you'll prosper. A REIT can run onto the rocks in numerous ways, including inept management, excessive overhead, risky or careless investments, overextension of resources, high development costs, and failures by borrowers or partners. There also are the dangers of such developments and conditions as those that apparently caused the decline—namely, high interest rates that discourage borrowing and construction, skyrocketing construction costs, builder defaults, an economic slowdown that cuts into the revenue of tenants and borrowers, a falloff in demand for new buildings of all types, and other factors outside the control of REIT managers.

Especially in its smaller form, a trust can be a device to conceal the identities of owners and investors, such as for the purpose of secretly including public officials and other influential persons. Trusts also are vulnerable to embezzlement and other fraud schemes by their managers to divert investors' money into their own pockets or to secretly owned companies.

Distinguishing Good Groups from Bad Groups

Some forms of group investing can be useful to the small investor, especially small groups in which he can exercise some control over the extra power that's gained. Taking on a few partners to take advantage of an otherwise unreachable opportunity for big profits can be a resourceful move.

But, compared to most group investing, especially in large groups where your share of the action is small, your influence nil, and your profits relatively small, raw land has much greater appeal.

14

OPTIONS AND
OTHER WAYS TO INVEST
AT NO COST OR RISK

One way to get rid of all risk in selling land is to sell it before you buy it.

That happens partially when you sell land before you complete a purchase on a land contract or a mortgage, and it's a key element in credit leverage. The less of the purchase price you pay before you sell, the greater your leverage. But, in buying that way, you make a commitment to purchase, pay part of the price, and are obligated to make additional payments until you sell.

To sell land before you pay any of the purchase price, you can use a handy device known as an option—a right to buy at a specified price for a certain period of time. In an option, the owner obligates himself to sell if you choose to buy, but you are not obligated to buy if you decide not to. It's your choice.

If you can find a buyer who agrees to a higher price before your option expires, you exercise it. If not, you let it lapse.

If you spot a $50,000 piece of land that's available for $40,000, for instance, but it takes $8,000 to swing the deal and you have only $1,000, you might save the deal with an option. You approach the owner with a proposal to buy if he'll give you a six-month option for $500, because you need the time to raise the money. If he agrees, you start looking for a buyer. Since you have the option to buy at $40,000, he cannot legally sell to anyone else until the option expires.

When to Use an Option to Get the Best Odds

There is, of course, a drawback. You lose the $500 if you don't come up with a buyer in time, or the rest of the money. You may decide it's worth gambling $500 on a chance to make a quick $10,000. But don't forget it's a gamble.

You can improve your odds, however, by using such a ploy only when you have a likely buyer already lined up, or you're reasonably sure you can otherwise come up with the funds to complete the purchase. Most options provide that if you exercise them, the amount paid for the option is applied to the purchase price.

Using Options as a Route to Rezoning Profits

Options can be a useful device in situations where you believe there's a good chance of getting a rezoning that will produce a profitable value jump, but where you can't or don't want to stake a lot of money on it.

For instance, you can buy a $20,000 parcel for $5,000 down and figure it would be worth $50,000 if you could get it rezoned commercial. But if you can't get it rezoned quickly, the prospects for a quick value rise are remote. So you'd rather gamble $500 on an option than tie up $5,000 and subsequent payments, unless there's a house or another income-producing structure on the land. But even then you can try an option first, putting off a purchase decision until you see what happens to your rezoning application.

The Real Estate Listing as an Option

Real estate agents automatically get many opportunities to make use of the option tactic. Instead of just acting as the seller's agent when a good buy comes along, they can buy the real estate, themselves, using their commission as all or part of the down payment. Then they resell at a higher price.

But, they don't have to buy before they resell, because a listing is in effect a form of option. Since the seller commits himself in the listing agreement to sell at a certain price, he in effect is granting everyone an option to buy at that price for the period of the listing.

The agent who sees a chance to make more by buying and reselling than he can in a sales commission, whether he be the listing agent or another agent, can look for a buyer at a higher price rather than the listing price. If he finds one, he buys at the lower listing price, himself, and resells. All he's invested is his time and effort.

You theoretically can do the same thing, since you have just as much right to buy at the listing price as an agent. However, you don't have as much ready access to buyers, and you couldn't sell through another agent what you don't already own or have an exclusive right to buy. While you're looking for a buyer, someone else can buy the land ahead of you. The agent is subject to the same risk, but he's not gambling much because he's looking for a buyer, anyway, even if only to make a commission.

No-Cost Options and Other No-Risk Gambits

A sounder way to reduce or eliminate the cost and any risk of loss is to get an option at no cost, or only a nominal cost of $1 or $10. This can sometimes be done by persuading a seller you need time to come up with the money but hesitate to make the effort to get the money if there's a danger that he will sell to someone else in the meantime.

Another approach is to substitute other consideration for cash. You can offer the seller, in return for a six-month option, a portion of any profit you make through resale to a buyer known only to you or through development of the land.

There may be several things you can offer instead of cash, such as business or professional services or even an agreement to make improvements on the property.

A no-risk approach that's similar to an option, but in many ways better, is the contingency contract, in which the agreement to purchase is contingent, or dependent, upon a subsequent occurrence or condition. If the contingency fails to develop, you are not obligated to go ahead with the purchase. If you have control over the contingency, the contract in effect becomes a free option.

The need for cash is not eliminated, since you ordinarily must make a deposit of up to $1,000 on a purchase contract or offer as earnest money. But all or most of the risk is gone. If the deal falls through because a contingency is not satisfied, you get the deposit back. Of course, you can have a no-cash deal if you borrow the $1,000 in the first place.

Contingency contracts are quite common. When you sign an agreement or an offer to buy a house with a mortgage loan, you probably are signing a contingency contract. Such an agreement or offer almost always contains a contingency provision that you're not obligated to buy if you can't get approval for a mortgage loan of a specified amount.

A Variety of Uses and Big Profits with No Risk

Contingency contracts are useful in all kinds of real estate investments. They can take many forms, and the kinds of possible contingencies are unlimited. You can make a purchase agreement contingent on your being able to borrow or otherwise raise a specified amount of money, on approval of a zoning change or construction permits, on the execution of certain agreements with other parties, on your ability to secure improvements at satisfactory cost, on the seller's performing certain improvements or providing title insurance, and so on. I even know of purchase agreements made contingent on the buyer's being able to find another buyer for resale.

An investor in Dayton, O., a few years ago put a $1,000 deposit on a

$275,000 purchase contract for a 12-acre parcel in a suburban area, with the contract contingent on his obtaining another buyer to build apartments. Before completing his purchase, he contracted to sell a small piece of the land to a chain restaurant company for $80,000 and the rest for $250,000 to an organization that wanted to build apartments. All the purchases were closed on the same day, 17 months after the original contract was signed, with the original owner deeding the land directly to the restaurant firm and the apartment builders. The first buyer never held title to the land. But he made a profit, after paying commissions and other expenses, of $44,000—a nifty return of 4,400 percent on his $1,000 investment in only 17 months, with absolutely no risk of loss whatsoever.

In another case, a real estate broker agreed to buy a run-down apartment complex contingent on his negotiating a contract to renovate the apartments and resell them to the local housing authority. He secured the agreement with the housing authority, then made the purchase. He didn't put any money into the apartments until his profits of more than $100,000 were assured. Actually, he didn't need any cash at all. Once he had the contract with the housing authority, he was able to borrow whatever he needed.

It's also common to make purchase contracts contingent on the obtaining of lease contracts from prospective tenants when buying improved real estate.

Tactics for No-Money-Down Investments

Obtaining lease contracts in advance is also a way to buy existing buildings with no initial investment, since you may be able to use them as collateral to borrow whatever funds you need to make the purchase.

Some of these tactics make you a promoter or a developer as well as an investor, and they take more time and effort than just buying and waiting. But they are effective techniques for making money on little or no investment at low risk. They also can be more challenging and invigorating than just waiting for appreciation to build, especially if they enable you to pyramid your profits faster.

Another way to buy improved property with no down payment is to get a mortgage loan for the total amount of a below-market purchase price. I've known several people who operate that way regularly. If an apartment house or small store is for sale at $40,000, they offer $30,000 because that's the amount they can borrow from a bank. If they can't buy it for that, they don't buy it. They keep making offers like that until someone accepts. Then they sell it for the market price. Many investors buy and sell houses that way.

This almost always requires, however, an already established connection with a bank or other mortgage lender, either through past mortgage business or other dealings. The bank gives you an exemption from the ordinary practice of lending no more than a certain percent—60 to 80 perhaps—of the purchase price, not the market value. Ordinarily, if the price is $30,000 and the mortgage loan percentage is 75, you could borrow no more than $22,500, regardless of whether the market value is $40,000.

For you to get a loan for 75 percent of $40,000 when the purchase price is only $30,000, you need the approval of a top bank official or a majority of a bank's loan committee. That doesn't happen if you're a stranger, an infrequent customer, or even a regular depositor with no prior experience in such dealings. Among the advantages that real estate agents enjoy in making investments of their own is that they have a chance to acquire such a banking connection in the normal course of arranging real estate financing for others.

An established connection or line of credit with a bank or two—or other lenders—can be especially valuable in enabling you to get low prices by paying cash. If you can get a $25,000 piece of vacant land for $10,000 because the seller is anxious for cash, the ability to borrow it quickly gives you the power to swing the deal.

Double Borrowing for No-Cash Deals

A variation on the theme of borrowing the entire purchase price is to borrow from two sources, which can be done regardless of the price. Here are some ways to do this:

1. Assume an existing mortage and borrow the difference between the mortgage balance and the purchase price, on a second mortgage or other type of loan. The drawback here is that interest rates on second mortgages and most other loans are high, which increases the risk that costs may exceed income.

2. Execute two new mortgages to raise the total purchase price. This method is ordinarily usable only with improved land, but some states may permit banks to make mortgage loans on raw land.

3. Buy a vendee's interest in a land contract, borrowing what you need to pay the difference between the contract balance and the purchase price.

4. Borrow the money you need for a down payment on a land contract or mortgage.

5. Make a separate agreement to cover a down payment with a consideration other than cash, such as a share in future profits or income.

A Combination Maneuver to Buy with No Money

A unique method of making an investment without cash is to make combined use of two devices—the partnership and the real estate agent's commission. You take in the real estate agent as a partner and he uses his commission to reduce the price and perhaps cover the entire down payment. You may put up an equal amount, or whatever more is needed for the down payment, depending on your partnership agreement.

But sometimes you can get your agent partner to let you contribute to the partnership in some other way while his commission takes care of the down payment. That might take the form of giving him a bigger share of the profit, contributing your work and services, having a likely prospect for sale already lined up, or giving him a share of another property you own.

This useful technique is more likely to be possible when you know a real estate agent with whom you have dealt regularly.

Opportunities at Rock-Bottom Prices

Much land can be bought at low prices from sources that tend to be overlooked.

One that most people have heard about is the local tax sale or sheriff's auction in which real estate is sold because the property taxes are delinquent. In times of economic recession or depression, it's sometimes possible to buy valuable or potentially valuable land for as little as the amount of the overdue taxes. Many people lost property during the Great Depression of the 1930's because they couldn't pay the taxes, and many others became rich in later years because they were able to buy land at tax sales in the 1930's.

In prosperous times, however, good land is hard to get that way. Few people are forced by conditions to let good land get away from them. Most of what's sold at tax auctions is inferior land or property that's not usable, and there's much competition for the few good pieces. Yet, you can run into a sleeper sometimes if you are alert to promising properties on the delinquent tax rolls and check them out carefully before the sale. You can find out about tax sales and when they are held by contacting the local tax collection office (usually the municipal or county treasurer's office).

There are many other kinds of government land sales, too. Though it's seldom publicized and not widely known, agencies on all levels of government sell land, usually by auction or sealed bid. Practically any governmental department, division, bureau, agency, commission or board can buy and dispose of land.

A state highway department, for instance, or a city transit authority sometimes sells surplus land—land it bought or condemned but didn't use, or land it formerly used but no longer needs. Or you might find a good vacation-land investment among tracts sold by a state agency such as Natural Resources or Conservation that oversees state wilderness lands. Minimum prices ordinarily are set according to an appraisal, but sometimes you can find a true steal, a piece of land whose high profit potential has been overlooked by everyone else.

Information on land sales by state agencies can be obtained by writing to state departments of Highways, Natural Resources, State Lands, Conservation, Public Lands, or General Services.

Good Buys from Our Largest Landowner, Uncle Sam

Opportunities for low-price, good quality land in undeveloped areas can be found among agencies of the federal government, where more than half of the government's lands—some 482 million acres—are controlled by the Bureau of Land Management.

The Bureau of Land Management sells land in large isolated tracts and mountainous tracts. U.S. citizens may also buy up to five acres under the Small Tract Act. The Desert Land Act provides for sale of up to 230 acres at $1.25 an acre in 13 Western states to individuals who irrigate and cultivate a portion. The Bureau of Land Management also sells land at auction. As mentioned in an earlier chapter, it sold 1,700 acres of Arizona and California land at an average price of $75 per acre in a recent year, and more than 9,000 at an average of $37 an acre in Nevada. Free land is available under the Homestead Act to heads of families over 21 years old who do not own more than 160 acres of U.S. land and who locate on the land. However, there is little homestead land available except in remote areas of Alaska, and the homesteader must farm the land seven months a year for three years to keep it, bearing the cost himself of clearing the land, or farm 10 of the 160 acres for one year and pay $1.25 an acre. It's also possible in some circumstances to gain title to public land by discovering a valuable mineral on it and mining it. Information on all these and others can be obtained by writing to the Bureau of Land Management, Department of Interior, Washington, D.C. 20240.

The Bureau of Reclamation also sells homesteads and land on irrigation projects. The General Services Administration sells excess land throughout the United States for several federal agencies. The U.S. Department of Housing and Urban Development conducts many property disposal sales each year, including nursing homes, apartments and single-family homes, though these are usually distressed properties that have been repossessed.

Information on tax sales and other government land auctions can also be found in the classified sections of newspapers. There you will see, in addition, notices of auctions by private owners who are disposing of real estate because of bankruptcy, foreclosure, divorce, litigation, liquidation of an estate, or other reason.

Whenever you think of buying land at an auction, be sure to investigate the property in advance, decide on the top bid at which it's a good buy, and don't let yourself be stampeded over that amount by the excitement of the bidding (if it's not a sealed bid sale).

Selling Land to the Government

Government is a potential buyer of land, too. In a growing suburban area, the board of education is looking for school sites, for instance. If you have a few vacant acres or can buy some that might make a suitable site, this is an application of the fringe buying technique to remember. It's not hard to find out where population growth indicates more schools will be needed; the school board and local planning boards have such information.

I know a former real estate man and farmer, now retired, who made a bundle by buying up land and selling it a few years later to the local school board. He was aided by friends in school board politics who knew where new schools would be needed.

It's a common tactic among people in the know on the location of new public facilities like schools, roads and airports to buy up land in those areas secretly—sometimes under the names of relatives or corporations—before the public knows about the projects. They know they will make a profit when the government agency comes along to buy their land.

Some do this because they have, or believe they can get access to, enough political influence to get high prices. Though government usually must follow strict rules when selling real estate or when buying anything else, it often has a great deal of leeway in the purchase of real estate. There are usually no sealed competitive bid requirements; real estate can be bought by negotiation. If the government tries to get a low price, the landowner can refuse to sell or have a chance at a higher price from a condemnation jury. But if the government pays a high price, no one blocks it.

However, this can be speculation rather than investing, and of dubious propriety. Someone else may have more political clout than you. Instead of condemning, the school board may look elsewhere. Government agencies often change their plans, such as the way they moved that interchange 300 feet to the north to cut off all the road frontage on my parcel near Detroit.

That's also treading on the edge of improper conduct, since it's public money that's involved, and it's easy to get caught, since the expenditure of public money is subject to public audit and is a matter of public record open to inspection and investigation by the news media.

It's not recommended that you play the influence game, either in locating land in the path of public projects or in running up the price you get. If you sell real estate to a governmental unit, operate in a straightforward, aboveboard manner.

Something for the Adventurous Types

One last trick for those who like a gamy lifestyle: *other-than-monthly* land contract payments. If you can make annual or semi-annual payments—or at any other interval—instead of monthly payments, you get more time to sell your land before the next payment comes due and you have to shell out more money. This prolongs your leverage effects, and may enable you to put in less total money—even though an annual lump sum payment costs you a bit more than 12 monthly payments due to a higher interest cost.

For instance, if you buy $10,000 worth of land with $1,500 down and agree to pay $1,000 at the end of each year, but sell after 22 months, you get a 10-month free ride, except for interest costs. On the other hand, having to make such a large payment may seem a lot harder to do than 12 little ones, even though it was nice while it was being deferred.

As a variation on this theme, it's sometimes possible to keep monthly payments low by providing for a "balloon" payment of a large portion of the price after several years or at the end of a land contract—for instance, $80 a month for five years and $5,000 at the end of that time. This gives you five years to sell without investing much.

Another variation is to put payments off altogether for several years, just paying interest in the meantime. I know of a $1.2 million purchase by an investment group under an agreement that allowed six years before the first payment on the mortgage came due. Before the six years was up, they resold enough of the land to more than cover the payment.

This is quite an adventurous approach, of course, since you face the danger that the investment will fare poorly and you will find yourself coming up fast on the due date without the money you need and no easy way to get it.

15

WHY RAW LAND IS
THE BEST WAY TO INVEST

To become a prosperous lawyer or doctor, you must master a long, rigorous course of study and struggle through many lean years while you build a practice.

To become a high-salaried corporation executive, you must contribute long years of 16-hour-a-day dedication and ruthlessly subordinate other interests to company loyalty.

To become a successful businessman, you must put in endless days of grueling work and be blessed with healthy doses of luck.

To do well enough in any profession or occupation to build a secure and comfortable life for yourself and your family, you must get an education or serve an apprenticeship, then work hard for a lifetime while contriving to spend less on ever-increasing living expenses than you earn—in short, be a magician.

The Easiest Path to Wealth and Security

But, to make lots of money in real estate, you don't have to do any of those things first. You don't need a college degree or a training program. You don't need an impressive list of qualifications. You don't need to pass a test, get a license, or obtain anyone's permission. Investing in real estate is the easiest thing in the world and it's open to everyone. All you need to do is go out and do it.

If there's information or knowledge you need in order to invest prudently and astutely, you're free to go out and get that, too.

You don't need to be a member of the local country club or be in good graces with the community power structure. You aren't dependent on the help or approval of any person or organization. You don't have to be wealthy, prominent or well-connected. There's no requirement that you please any clique or kow-tow to any powerful people. If you want to invest in a piece of land, no one can stop you. No one will even try to.

An Investment for the Modern-Day Individualist

A recent report by a nationally prominent opinion polling firm said Americans are less confident than ever that they can control their own destinies. The rugged American individualist is vanishing, said the report, and in his place stands a nervous, fearful citizen who feels powerless to cope with the complex obstacles of modern life and is growing increasingly dependent on his government and his employer. According to the report, people no longer believe that the individual can get what he wants on his own initiative.

Investing in real estate, however, is one way you can still exercise your individualism and be the master of your own fate. Real estate remains as much as ever an opportunity for individual initiative, action, and success.

In no other kind of endeavor can a person of modest means act with such freedom, self-reliance and ease. You don't have to get rich before you can invest successfully in real estate. You can use real estate to get rich. Your family's security need not hang on the whim of a boss or the business acumen of your employer. You can use real estate to provide your own security.

Building a Fortune as a Part-Time Pursuit

You don't need to slave and save half your life to get a nest egg for comfortable retirement, send your children to college, or take a trip to Europe. You can build a fortune in just a few years in your spare time, starting right now.

You don't have to quit your job or work long hours on evenings and weekends. You can make big profits in real estate on the side, without distracting you from your main occupation, career or interests, and without taking more than a few hours when you feel like it.

Making money in real estate is so easy to do, and so easy to learn how to do, that you can build yourself a fortune as a part-time pursuit.

Why Real Estate Is the Best Investment

How easy it is, nevertheless, is just one reason why real estate is the best way to invest, especially for the small investor. Here are the other main reasons:

1. Low Risk

Since the value of real estate's main ingredient, land, is more stable and more predictable than any other investment, it's also safer. Land is far more certain than any other investment to increase in value, due to the natural limit on supply and the inevitability of increasing demand. Land will never go out of style.

Other investments—common stocks, securities, mutual funds, business ventures, commodities, precious metals and others—will always fluctuate in value under the impact of changing circumstances and attitudes. They are always subject to the danger of becoming worthless. A piece of land is always there; it doesn't disappear. You can make a mistake or two in land, or something unexpected can go wrong, and you still have a good chance of avoiding a loss or making some profit.

While land values kept rising in recent years, the value of most securities listed on the national stock exchanges took nosedives. So did mutual funds. In Las Vegas recently, the dealers, cashiers and change girls at the Lady Luck Casino refused to invest their profit-sharing funds in the stock market because they said it was too big a gamble.

Even an apparently secure investment like a savings account, a government bond or an insurance policy is actually less safe than land. The value of fixed returns on such investments can be wiped out by inflation, while land rises in value along with inflation and often faster. Besides, an insurance company, like any other company, can collapse.

You can lose money in real estate if you're careless or extraordinarily unlucky, but losses are easier to avoid than in any other kind of investment.

2. Big Profits

No other investment can match the potential return from prudent techniques. The only way you can do as well in the stock market or elsewhere is for lightning to strike with fantastic luck. You don't have to be lucky to make big money in real estate, just careful to use the techniques that take maximum advantage of land's natural tendency to rise in value rapidly in the face of imminent usage change.

Using low-price leverage and credit buying leverage, you can easily make 100, 200 and even 1,000 percent or more on your investment in a short time, and multiply that further with pyramiding techniques that compound the effects of appreciation. In any other form of investment, making 15 percent on your money is considered splendid. Moody's industrial stocks index showed an average return of only 7.3 percent per year over a recent 10-year period. Experts who say land must appreciate 12 to 14 percent per year to match other investment opportunities overlook the availability and effects of leverage.

Starting with $200 in 1967, I built an investment worth $50,000 to $60,000 in northern Michigan vacation land alone in only seven years.

3. Durability

Not only is real estate relatively immune to short-term vacillations in value, but land also is comparatively invulnerable to such perils as economic slumps, tight money, inflation, international conflicts, energy crises, and shortages of various kinds. Economic conditions do affect some forms of real estate, but not usually as severely as other investments.

Real estate values sometimes lie dormant for a while, or even decline in particular locations or circumstances. But such declines are usually temporary, and land, as something that does not go out of existence no matter how bad things get, always has a far better chance of surviving a crisis than any other investment. If its current use is no longer profitable, it's still there and always is potentially usable for something.

4. Tax Benefits

Federal income tax laws bestow more tax advantages on real estate investing than on any other form of investment. The depreciation tax shelters available on buildings, especially multiple-unit dwellings, can be found nowhere else.

Some other forms of investment, including securities, do have access to the lower capital gains rates on the sale of property held more than six months, but only in real estate can you spread these taxes over several years. This can be done by selling on a land contract or mortgage and receiving less than 30 percent of the sale price (in down payment and subsequent installments, not counting interest) in the year of the sale. This way you can declare each year only the amount of profit actually received that year, instead of declaring the total profit in the year of the sale. If enough money is involved to make a significant difference in your tax bracket, this advantage can increase your after-tax profits substantially.

Some forms of investment income get no capital gains rate benefits at all, such as interest on savings accounts and bonds. Interest on municipal bonds is tax free altogether, but this is an investment only for the already wealthy.

Why Raw Land Is the Best Real Estate for Investment

There are several reasons in addition, why raw land is the best kind of real estate for the investor, the easiest, safest, surest way of all to make big money with little risk:

1. Since there is more unused land than used land, there are more opportunities—and will be for many years to come.

2. Prices are lower, so it's easier to buy and there is greater leverage.

3. Since there are no structures, potential use is more flexible and there is more chance for fast, sharp value increases under the impact of approaching usage change.

4. Increases in value are more certain and there is less danger of value decline due to deterioration of neighborhood or other changes.

5. Though raw land ordinarily produces no income to offset costs, income property can end up costing more than it brings in.

6. Rental profits from improved real estate are taxable at ordinary rates on the federal income tax, just like dividends from stocks, whereas the chief source of profit in raw land—appreciation—is taxed at the lower capital gains rate.

7. The next best source of big profits in land, development, usually starts with raw land.

The Best Way to Start, the Best Way to Keep Going

Raw land is the best way to make big profits starting from scratch. Instead of needing to make money some other way so you can invest in real estate, you can make it first in land, and then have the money to try other ventures if you wish.

After you make a few high-profit deals, you may feel the urge to try other kinds of real estate or perhaps take a fling at the stock market, commodity futures or speculation in gold. But you can never invest in anything else that will give you the high odds for spectacular returns on low risk that you get in real estate.

Even after you're rolling in money from land investment exploits, real estate will still be the easiest, surest way to expand your wealth further—especially well-located raw land on the fringe of development.

A Few Other Benefits Besides Wealth

Real estate investing, as a surefire route to material enrichment for the independent, individualistic investor, can do even more for you than make money and express your individualism. It can also be a path to greater independence and self-reliance.

Real estate profits strengthen your ability to be independent in other aspects of life. Not only are you less dependent on your employer and the government for job security and retirement income, you can better afford to work at a career you enjoy but which doesn't pay much. You will be better able to pursue other goals like going back to school or making a contribution to society through involvement in politics, charity work or civic, cultural or artistic activities.

Real estate profits can be the wherewithal to improve the quality of your family's life, not just with increased material wealth and comfort, but also by reducing, for instance, your need to work long hours away from your family to make ends meet. You and your family will be able to enjoy more leisure time activities, more recreation, and more vacation trips.

Investing in real estate is also an ethical means to the attainment of comfort and security, an endeavor that's accepted and even admired in our society based on individual liberty and initiative in political, economic and social life.

You even make a contribution to the public welfare in the process of improving your own. The buying and selling of raw land may appear to serve no constructive or creative purpose, but you are converting the energy of a natural phenomenon—appreciation in value—into a social benefit as well as a personal one.

How One Man's Profits Can Benefit Others, Too

The value of land rises whether you enter the picture to buy and sell or not, but for each profitable transaction that occurs, a benefit accrues to at least one individual and probably several. This benefit not only causes some small positive impact on the local and overall economy, it also produces indirect benefits for society through the beneficial effects on individuals.

The more money you make and the more independent and self-sufficient it helps you become, the more buying power you and your family contribute to economic progress, the more effective and useful a citizen you become, and the more time and ability you have to serve the community through political, civic or cultural activities. You might even get time to write a great novel or produce a great painting.

The Greatest Benefit of All—Certainty of Success

Among all the benefits of investing in land, the one that stands out with the most vivid clarity and importance is the certainty that the benefits will continue to be accessible long into the future.

Not many things in life are certain—except, as the saying goes, death and taxes—and the history of mankind can be viewed as a story of man's search for certainty. But when it comes to the investment of time, energy, money or other resources, land comes as close to providing certainty of success as is possible.

As long as the world exists, so will land and so will opportunities to profit from it, no matter what course events may follow or how troublesome they threaten to be.

16

NO END IN SIGHT FOR
PROFIT OPPORTUNITIES

Land will always be man's most essential and most precious resource. Fashions in homes and styles of architecture change and different patterns of growth evolve, but underneath the varying details there is always one solid, unchangeable constant—land. Some land is more desirable, more valuable than other land, but all land has some potential use. Land will never become worthless.

Change is inevitable, but what changes in land is its use. Since usage change is the chief source of profit in raw land, opportunities for profit are also inevitable.

Unlimited Opportunities from a Limited Supply

The United States is still a young, growing country, with a great deal of uninhabited, unused land. Most usage change occurs in the development of raw land for its first use—single-family homes, apartments, vacation lots, shopping centers.

Continuing increases in population, affluence and economic growth will cause this kind of primary usage change to dominate real estate activity in America for at least another 50 years and probably a century or more. There may be short lulls, but over the long range this is the most predictable of economic eventualities. According to a report by the U.S. Senate Interior and Insular Affairs Committee, the nation will build as many homes, schools and hospitals in the next three decades as have been built in the past three centuries.

Even when overall demand slackens temporarily, there are pockets of growth and demand. There will always be some low-priced unused land coming into demand for development from the large but ultimately limited supply for many years to come.

Profits on the Fringe of Redevelopment

If the day should arrive hundreds of years from now that all land is used up, there will still be another kind of usage change with opportunities for profits; namely, redevelopment. Even today while suburbs are expanding faster than ever and vacation land is being developed at breakneck speed, many American cities have already entered the early stages of redevelopment usage change as they try to rebuild their old, deteriorated sections.

Slum redevelopment is bound to pick up momentum in the years ahead, bringing with it profit opportunities on its fringe similar to opportunities on the fringe of new development. If the nation's land were ever to be 100 percent developed, not only would land be more valuable than ever, but the inevitable changes would occur through redevelopment.

Whatever direction the future takes, there always will be plenty of chances for profit from the appreciation of land values under the impact of growing demand and approaching use change.

Opportunities on the fringe of redevelopment are already abundant in inner-city areas where land, either vacant or with rundown buildings, can be bought at distressed prices. One source is the U.S. Department of Housing and Urban Development, which disposes of repossessed homes, apartments and nursing homes. The drawback is that while eventual redevelopment of delapidated areas is inevitable, it's difficult to predict how soon it will happen.

Real estate on the fringe of redevelopment also is often still expensive even though it may have declined in value. Downtown land in most cities is still high priced despite the flight of residents and retailers to suburbia. According to Homer Hoyt, president of a real estate appraisal and analysis firm in Washington, D.C., there has been a "tremendous decline in land and building values in the ghettos occupied by black people in our northern cities," but central business land values "have remained stationary" or dropped only slightly, and "office building land values in central cities located in the direction of high income areas have increased to new high records."

This means it may be difficult for the small investor to get in on the profits from the coming redevelopment of urban areas, which, despite the emphasis so far on downtown revival, will probably follow a "multiple core" pattern in the future.

What the Multiple Core Pattern Will Look Like

Though urban redevelopment planners have largely been hung up on the old concept of a single downtown core for a metropolitan area, this concept is obsolete due to the increasingly enormous size of metropolitan areas and automobile traffic congestion.

It's futile for cities to focus all revitalization efforts on downtown areas. What's needed is several smaller cores—mini-downtown business and retail centers—scattered about the area. Downtown should be just one of several smaller cores instead of the only one.

Such multiple cores already exist in suburban areas, in the form of shopping centers. Some metropolitan areas like Los Angeles have developed in that fashion. For older cities to redevelop along such lines, more attention must be given to sections other than downtown and slum areas near downtown. This is sure to happen sooner or later, and when it does there will be investment opportunities on the fringes of these redevelopment areas.

Though such property probably will not be available at low prices, much of it may be obtainable with low down payments and produce income to carry the costs and pay for itself until a profitable resale can be made.

The Two Boom Areas of the Years Ahead

For the most part, however, the best investment opportunities over the next few decades are certain to remain concentrated in two areas:

1. Continued suburban expansion; and
2. Intensified growth in recreation, vacation and retirement property.

In addition to population growth and further technological and economic progress that will keep personal wealth and per capita demand for land on the rise, pressure for increased land use and rising values will come from continuing increases in automobile ownership, more highway construction, stepped up development of public parklands, new golf courses and other private recreation uses, efforts to develop new energy sources, environmental concerns, expanded land use controls, and an influx of foreign money.

The Non-Impact of the Energy Crisis

The recent energy crisis, with its soaring oil prices and threats of gasoline shortages, has shown no signs of slowing down suburban growth by discouraging commuting and reviving interest in urban living and mass transit, despite such predictions by some experts. Some even suspected that the feverish interest in recreation activities and vacation property would cool off. But that has not materialized, either.

Though the economy went into a slump, and growth into a stall, as reflected in mass layoffs of auto workers and a severe decline in the construction industry, there has been no evidence of less desire for suburban living or vacation land. The movement of business and industry to suburban locations has brought enough jobs outside the central cities that commuting distance is no longer a significant problem. The development of mass transit, in addition, would not necessarily retard the suburban exodus, and might even stimulate it by making commuting easier. Suburbanites would not have to drive all the way into the central city to work.

There's been evidence of less auto use, but no sign that it has translated into any diminishing of the crowds at ski lodges, or any let up in the demand for land. Many state governments are even moving ahead with plans for new highways as well as programs to help the construction industry.

If there has been any slackening in the demand for land, it has been slight. As in previous recessions, it was a good time to buy. Land values were sure to start a sharp new upcurve as soon as the economy recovered.

The Double-Edged Sword of Inflation

Meanwhile, inflation soars on unfazed by the energy crisis or the economic recession. Prices of just about everything will no doubt keep right on rising. There's no convincing evidence that inflation will be stopped or brought under control in the near future. Labor and materials will keep increasing in cost, making houses and other buildings more and more expensive—new structures directly and older ones indirectly.

The results will be twofold.

On one hand, high-density dwellings such as condominiums, town houses and apartments will become more popular. Their construction, heating and maintenance costs are less per square foot of living space than single-family homes. As a recent 278-page federal government report pointed out, the single-family home is the most expensive to build and the most inefficient to operate. The single-family home also uses more land per dwelling unit. An increased interest in multiple-unit living might tend to dampen the demand for land.

On the other hand, rising costs will push up the value of land, too. There will be more competition for multiple-unit sites. More commercial land will be needed near the high-density population of multiple-unit complexes. And those who live in apartments and condominiums will feel greater need for the use and ownership of recreation and vacation land. In any case, there will be plenty of land increasing in value.

The Price-Raising Effects of Government Action

Moves by federal, state, and local governments to develop more parks, campgrounds, and other recreation areas not only reduce the supply of land for private development, they increase the value of surrounding land. The search for more minerals and new energy sources also will increase the demand for land.

Steps by authorities at all levels to prevent soil erosion and other environmental damage by land developers, preserve ecologically valuable land and open space for public use, and impose antipollution controls, also push land prices up.

Developers who file environment impact statements, submit evidence of compliance with federal and state laws, or contest regulations in court, pass on the costs to buyers. The effect is to pull up the price of land, too. A recent ruling by the U.S. Environmental Protection Agency, for instance, requires developers of new apartments, shopping centers, office towers, residential subdivisions and industrial parks with parking for 1,000 or more cars to submit proof that their projects will not violate national air quality standards.

Many states have begun to impose tougher rules on vacation-land developers, especially in areas where local zoning codes and enforcement activities are lenient.

There's been burgeoning support for stronger controls on land use across the nation, an attitude that's reflected in the spread of regional planning commissions to regulate suburban growth (such as by confining commercial development to shopping center clusters instead of main road strips) and efforts in the U.S. Congress to enact a national land use law.

A proposed National Land Use Policy and Planning Assistance Act was passed by the U.S. Senate but failed to survive in the House of Representatives, though it no doubt will be revived. The bill would have appropriated $1.1 billion over eight years to help states plan and enforce land use controls. Some states have on their own begun to study the problem and enact land use legislation.

But more controls also mean more red tape and higher costs that put another upward pressure on land values. The supply of land that's acceptable for various uses is reduced, which makes it scarcer and more expensive. Furthermore, the clamor for controls tends to generate unwarranted fears of coming shortages in the public mind and the resultant anxiety to buy a vacation plot or a few acres before it's too late also drives up prices.

The Big New Town Flop

The move toward land use control has already run into a huge snag, however. The device envisioned as the chief instrument of planned, orderly growth in future years—the New Town—has run onto some rocks.

New Towns were conceived as totally planned new communities, with stores, offices, factories, schools, public buildings and other structures of a typical community planned in advance along with a residential mixture, instead of developing just the residential properties and letting everything else follow in traditional haphazard fashion. Development of utilities and public services is also included.

The idea originated many years ago with the building of Levittown, Pa., and Reston, Va., and gained momentum in recent years with the help of a U.S. Housing and Urban Development Department program to guarantee loans for planning, utility installation and construction. Several New Towns were started in various parts of America and many real estate experts began to see the concept—also called Planned Unit Development (PUD)—as a dream replacement for runaway suburban sprawl.

However, the dream has turned into a nightmare of red tape, bureaucratic disarray and financial calamity. A Dayton, O., area New Town of 4,000 acres called Newfields, for instance, has suffered mounting difficulties despite a special state law passed to smooth the way. Newfields has been plagued by a need to deal with several local governmental units that don't see eye to eye, a shortage of buyers for the first new homes to be built, and a delay in construction of new roads needed for convenient access.

Yet Newfields is well off compared to 14 other New Towns under construction across the nation with HUD-guaranteed loan money. Most of these have been facing financial collapse and even foreclosure. Near the end of 1974, it was learned that studies of the HUD program were critical of it. Then, early in 1975, HUD discontinued the New Town program, announcing it would accept no new applications. Since it's almost impossible to get financing without government guarantees for a project of such magnitude, HUD's action snuffed out the New Town dream, at least for a while.

Profits from Any Size Developer

The New Town idea would concentrate real estate development in the hands of big companies and big-money syndicates. Though the program's suspension might slow down that trend, real estate development will no doubt become more and more a big-business undertaking from now on, anyway.

However, it makes no difference to the small investor who isn't keen on being a developer in the first place. You can still buy land on the fringe of development and sell it to the developer when he gets there, or to someone else who will resell to the developer, regardless of whether the developer is big or small. You might even get a bigger price from a bigger developer.

The Impact of Foreign Money

Meanwhile, still more pressure on land values is being created by the influx of Arab oil money and other foreign investment funds into U.S. real estate. The

Arab oil nations alone have billions of dollars to invest and are looking for profitable places to put it.

A firm headquartered in the small principality of Kuwait has already bought an island off South Carolina, put up half interest in an Atlanta, Ga., hotel, and invested $50 million in office buildings, shopping centers and apartments through a Kentucky investment firm. The Shah of Iran reportedly bought a Fifth Avenue apartment building in New York City and a wealthy Saudi Arabian has purchased a million dollars worth of California land.

Nor are the Arabs alone. Japanese, Italian, German, Australian and other foreign investors have been pouring money into American real estate from their newly prosperous economies. As their economies continue to grow and the world's less advanced nations develop, still more foreign money will join the many forces that keep driving the value of American land upward.

Opportunity's Only Direction—Up

Changes in federal, state, and local tax policies may decrease depreciation writeoffs or the deductability of interest expenses, or raise property taxes, but there's nothing on the horizon that's likely to halt the rise in land values or diminish your opportunity to make big money by picking the right spots on the fringe of growth.

Every age tends to perceive itself as at the peak of progress. But the truth is just the opposite. Whatever has already happened, more growth, progress and opportunity lies ahead than has already taken place in the history of the world.

How long the current land boom lasts doesn't really matter. Short-range booms can come and go, but the long-range direction is inexorably up. Land will always be in demand. There will always be opportunities for profit from its rising value for anyone who goes and gets it. It's up to you.

INDEX